RALPH SANDER

PILGRIM'S PROGRESS

THE GRAPHIC NOVEL

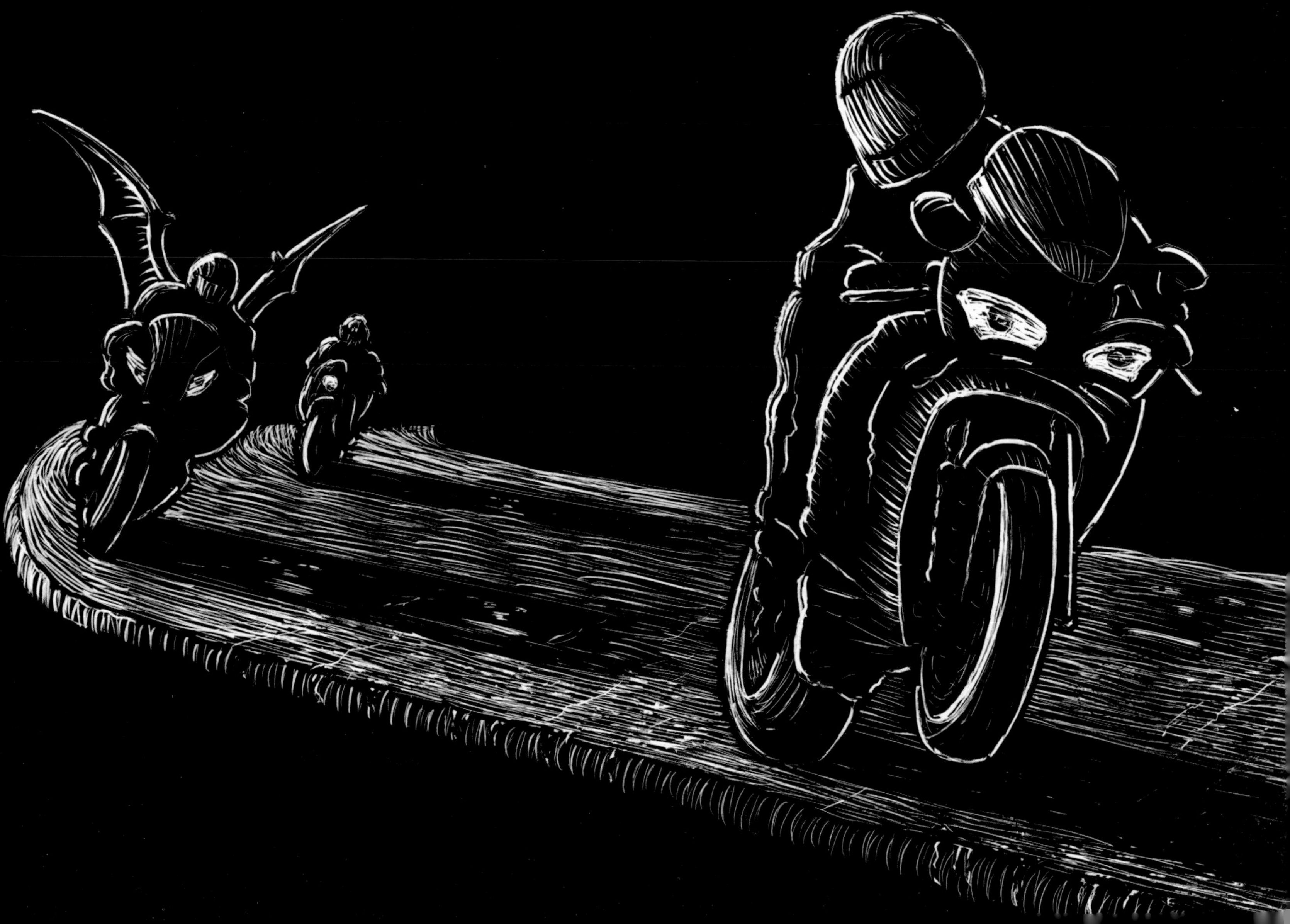

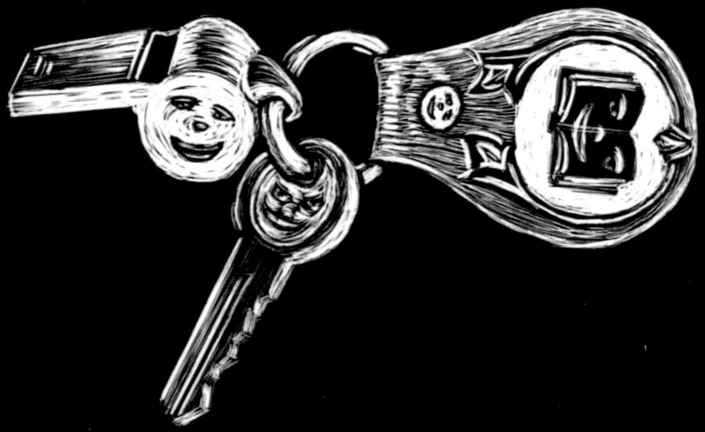

WHISTLE KEY BOOKS
P.O. Box 1771
Santa Cruz, California 95060-1771

Publisher: Ralph Sanders

First printing January 2018
ISBN: 978-0-692-99707-9
Printed in China

To my Mom, Ida Genelle; my wife, Francis Anne; my son, Joseph, and his wife, Jenn; my daughter, Rosemary; my brothers, Mike, Robert, David, and Charles. Those who have a child, brother, sister, aunt, uncle, niece, nephew with Down's Syndrome. Motorcycle riders. And especially all the people of the world trying to find their way to Heaven on all these roads lined with doors to Hell.

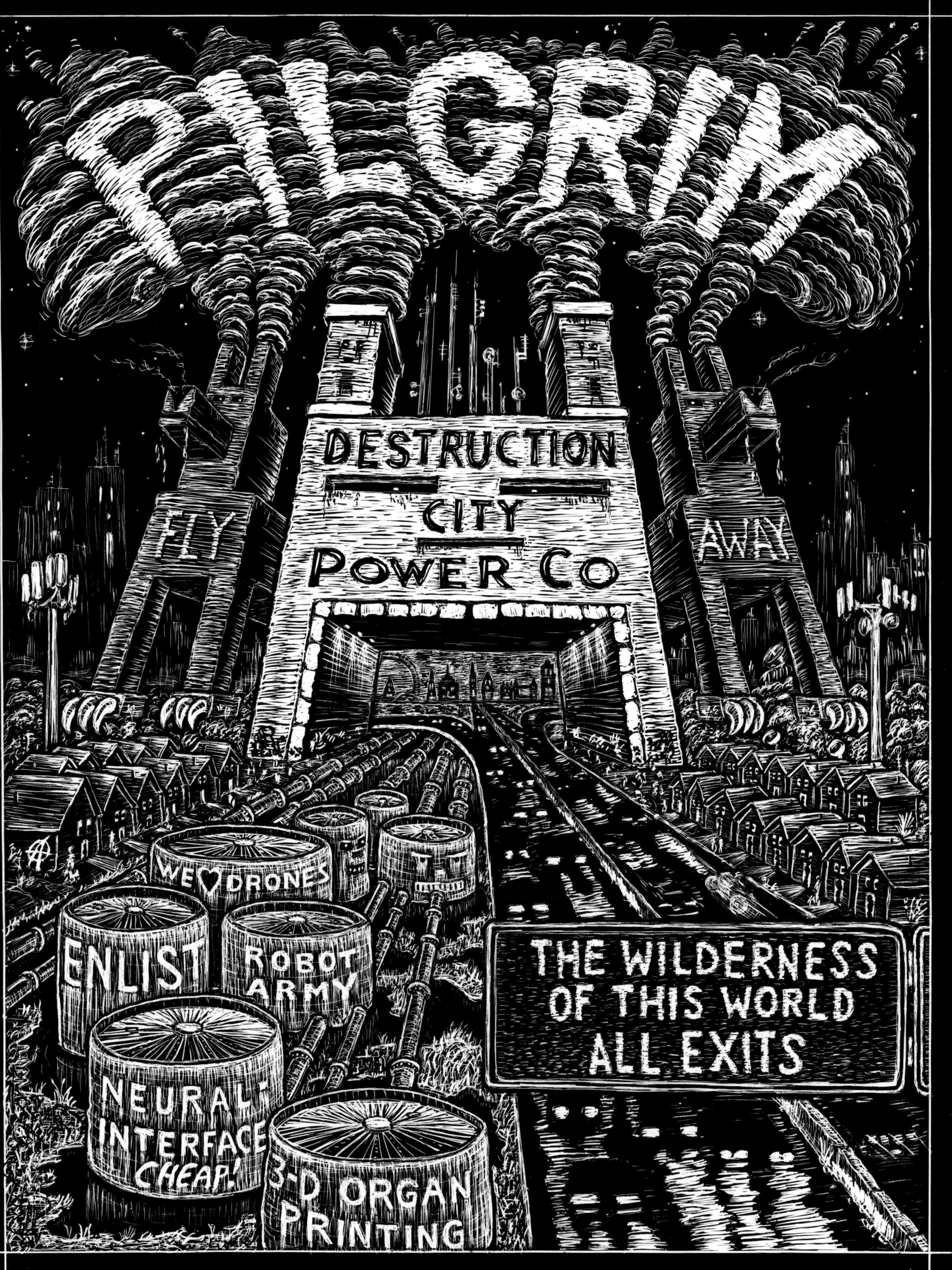
PILGRIM
DESTRUCTION
CITY
POWER CO
FLY
AWAY
WE ♡ DRONES
ENLIST
ROBOT ARMY
NEURAL-INTERFACE CHEAP!
3-D ORGAN PRINTING
THE WILDERNESS OF THIS WORLD
ALL EXITS

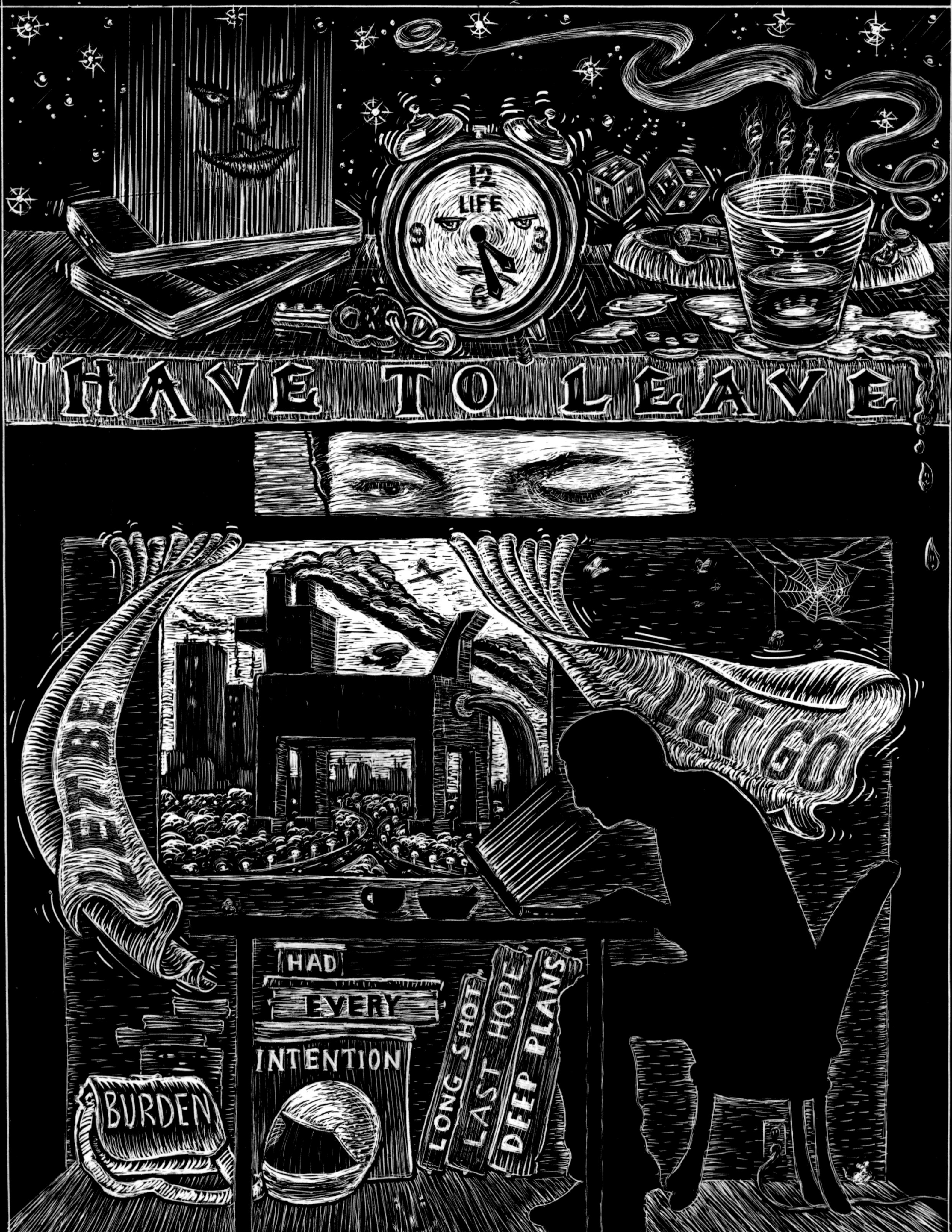
LIFE
HAVE TO LEAVE
LET BE
LET GO
HAD
EVERY
INTENTION
BURDEN
LONG SHOT
LAST HOPE
DEEP PLANS

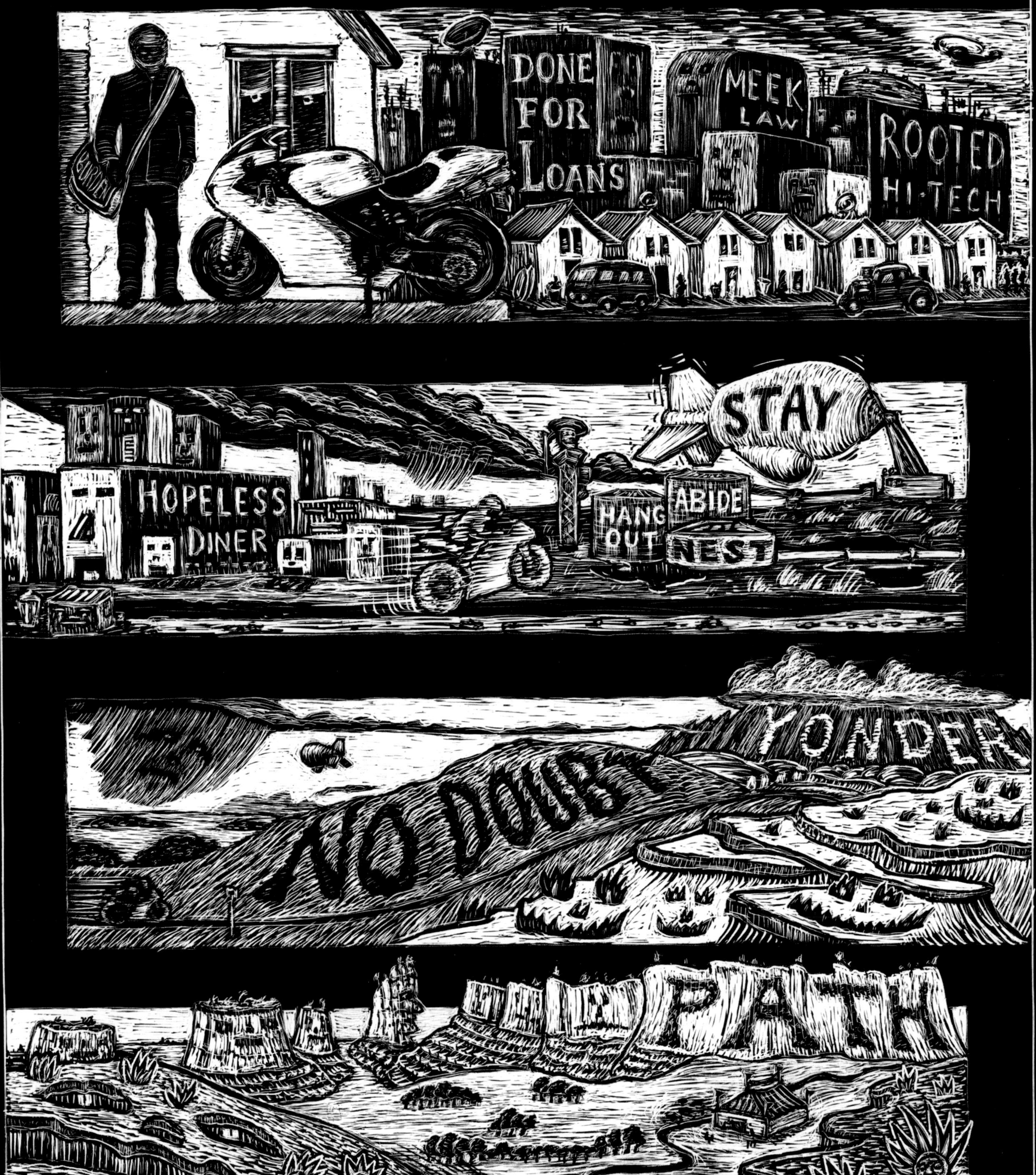
DONE FOR LOANS
MEEK LAW
ROOTED HI-TECH
HOPELESS DINER
STAY
HANG OUT
ABIDE
NEST
NO DOUBT
YONDER
PATH

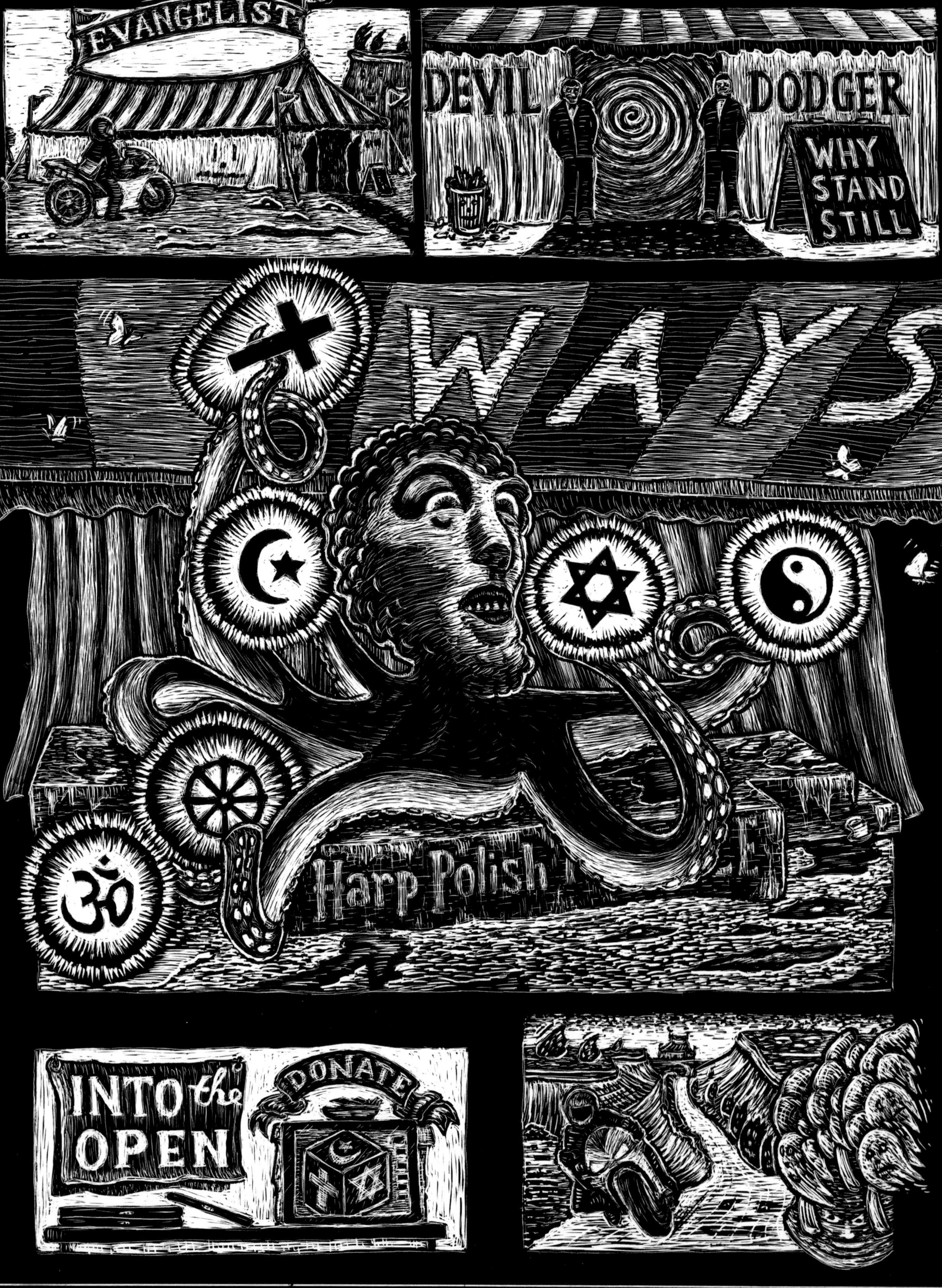
EVANGELIST
DEVIL
DODGER
WHY STAND STILL
WAYS
Harp Polish
INTO the OPEN
DONATE

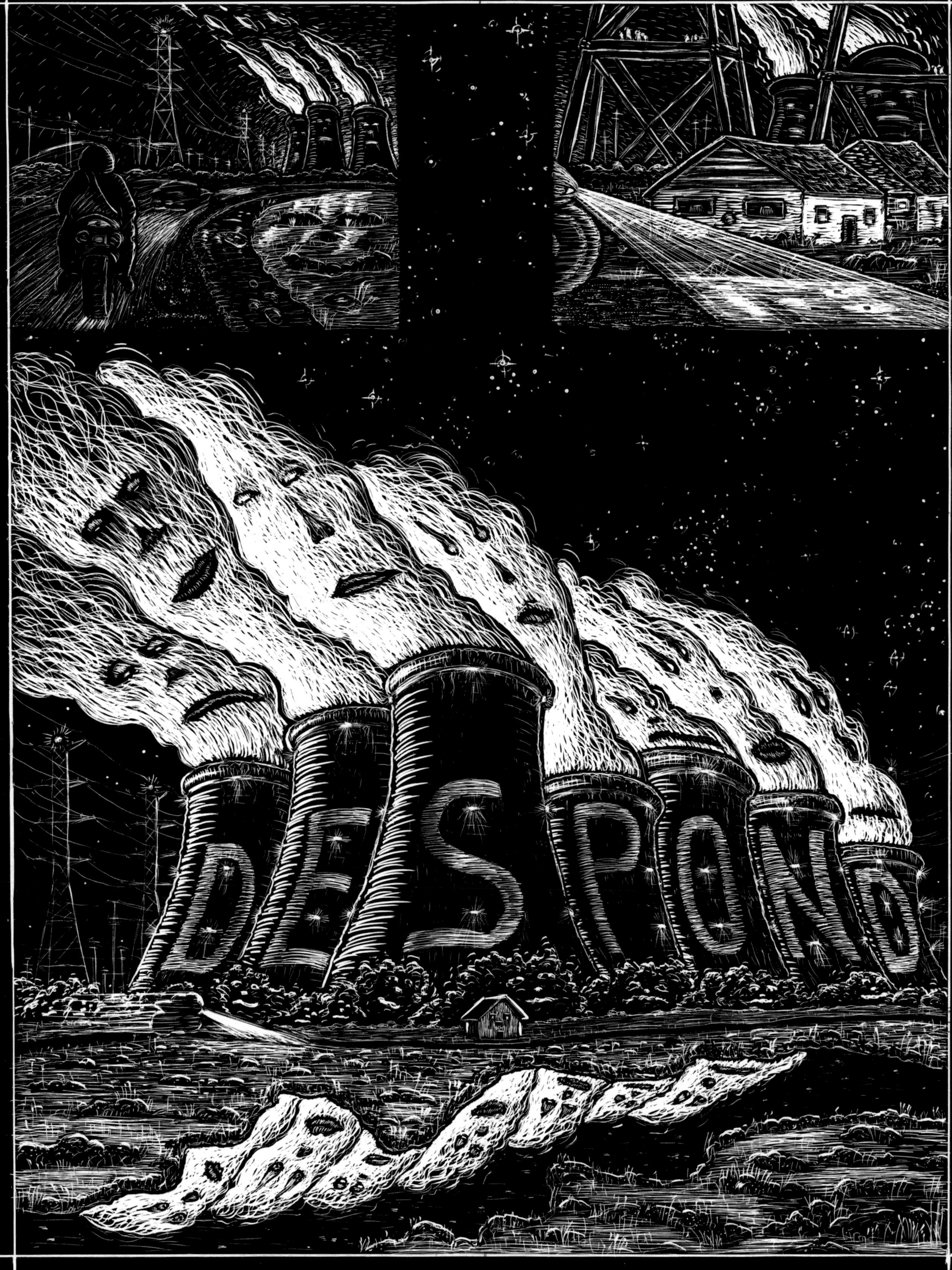
DESPOND

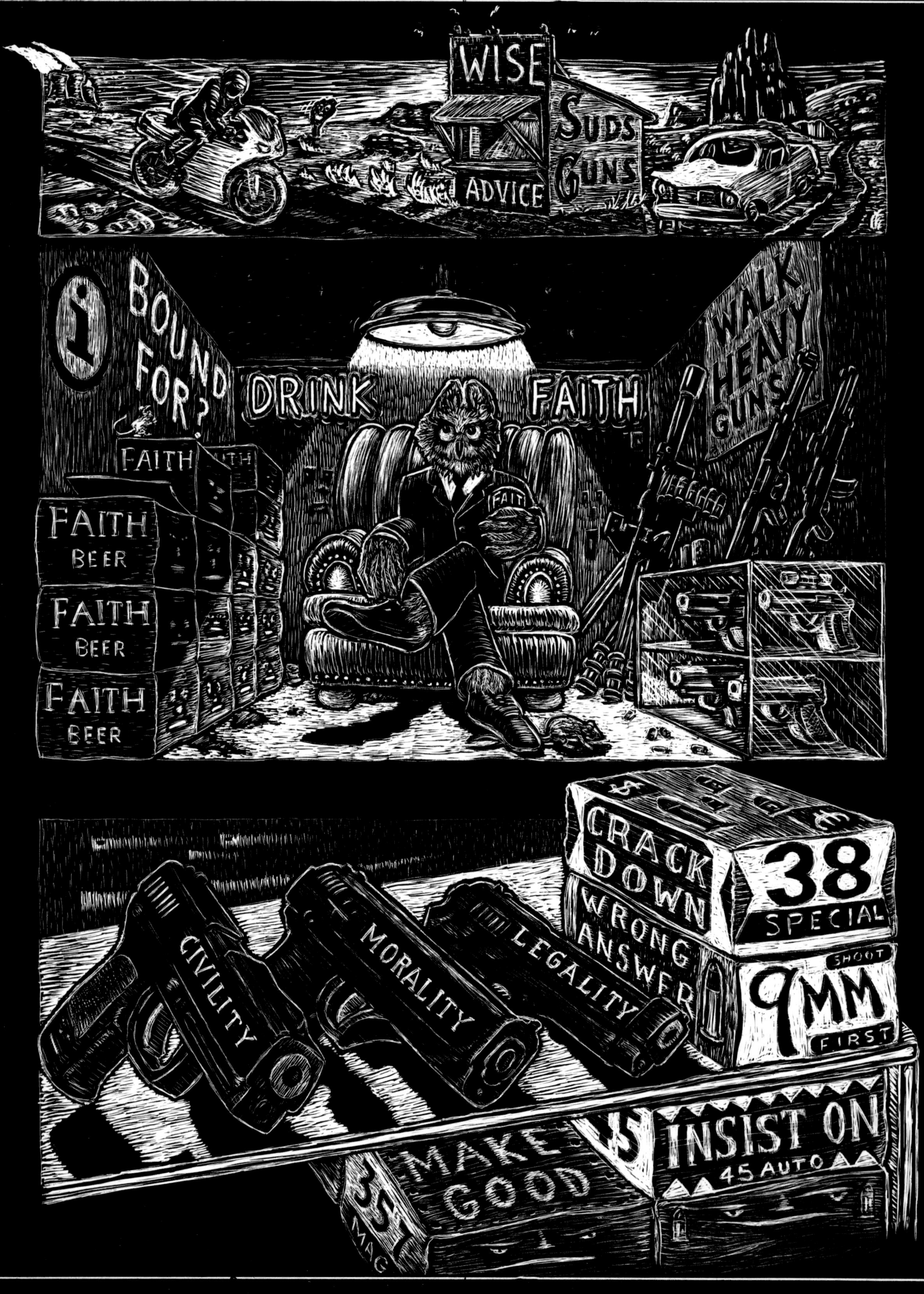
WISE
ADVICE
SUDS
GUNS
BOUND FOR?
DRINK
FAITH
WALK HEAVY
GUNS
FAITH
FAITH BEER
FAITH BEER
FAITH BEER
CRACK DOWN
38 SPECIAL
WRONG ANSWER
SHOOT 9MM FIRST
CIVILITY
MORALITY
LEGALITY
MAKE GOOD
357 MAG
INSIST ON
45 AUTO

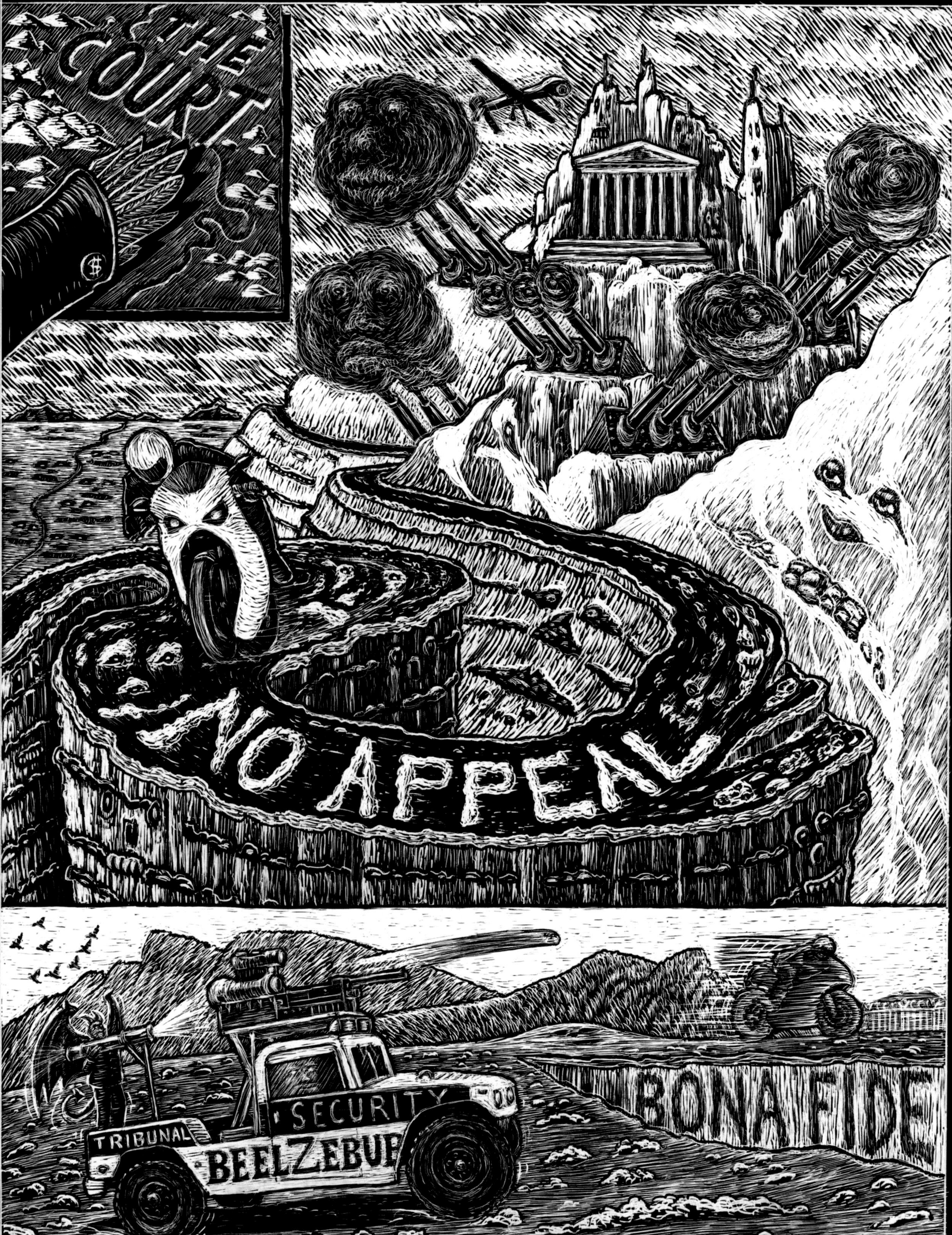
THE COURT
NO APPEAL
TRIBUNAL
SECURITY
BEELZEBUB
BONA FIDE

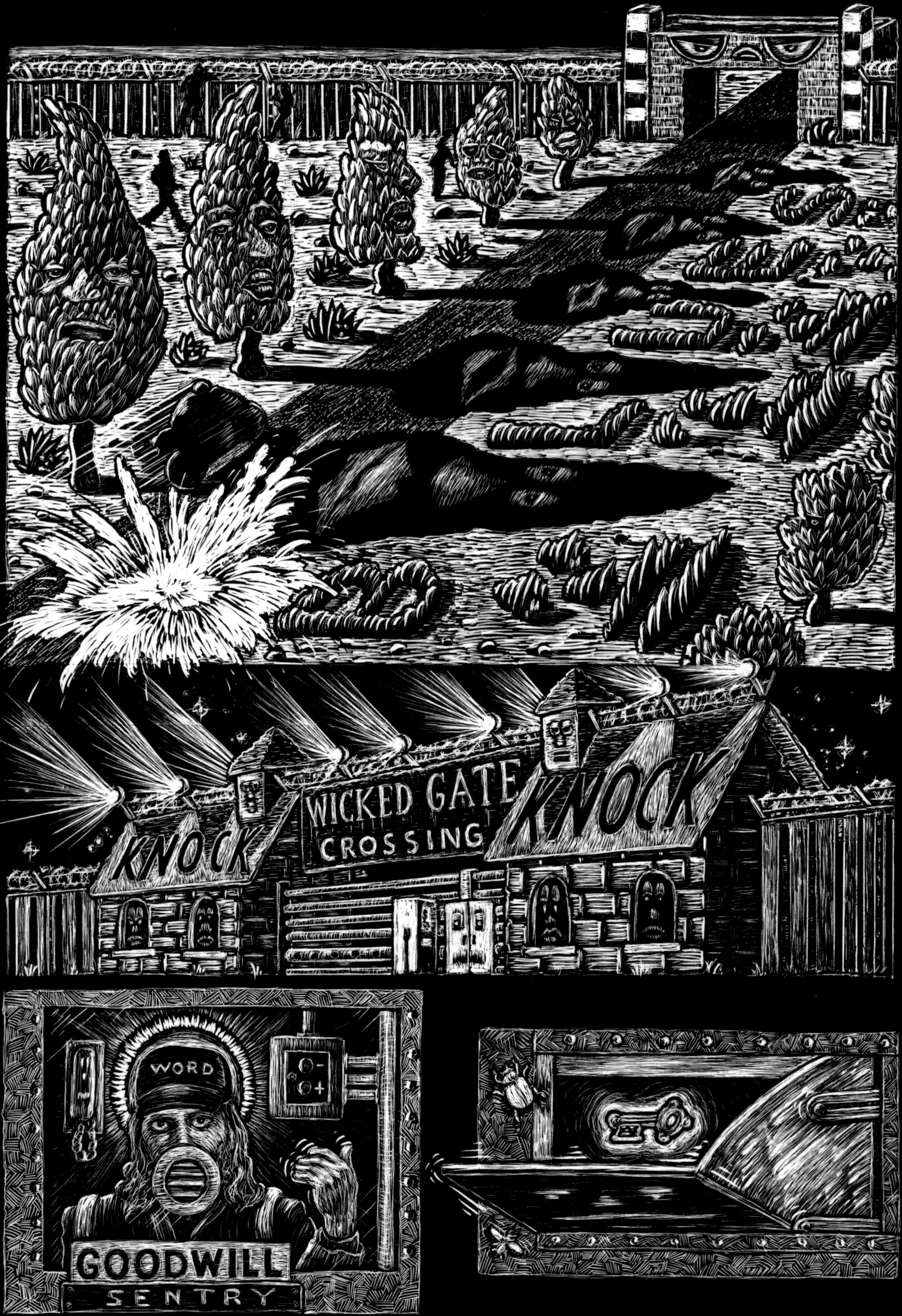
KNOCK
WICKED GATE
CROSSING
KNOCK
WORD
GOODWILL
SENTRY

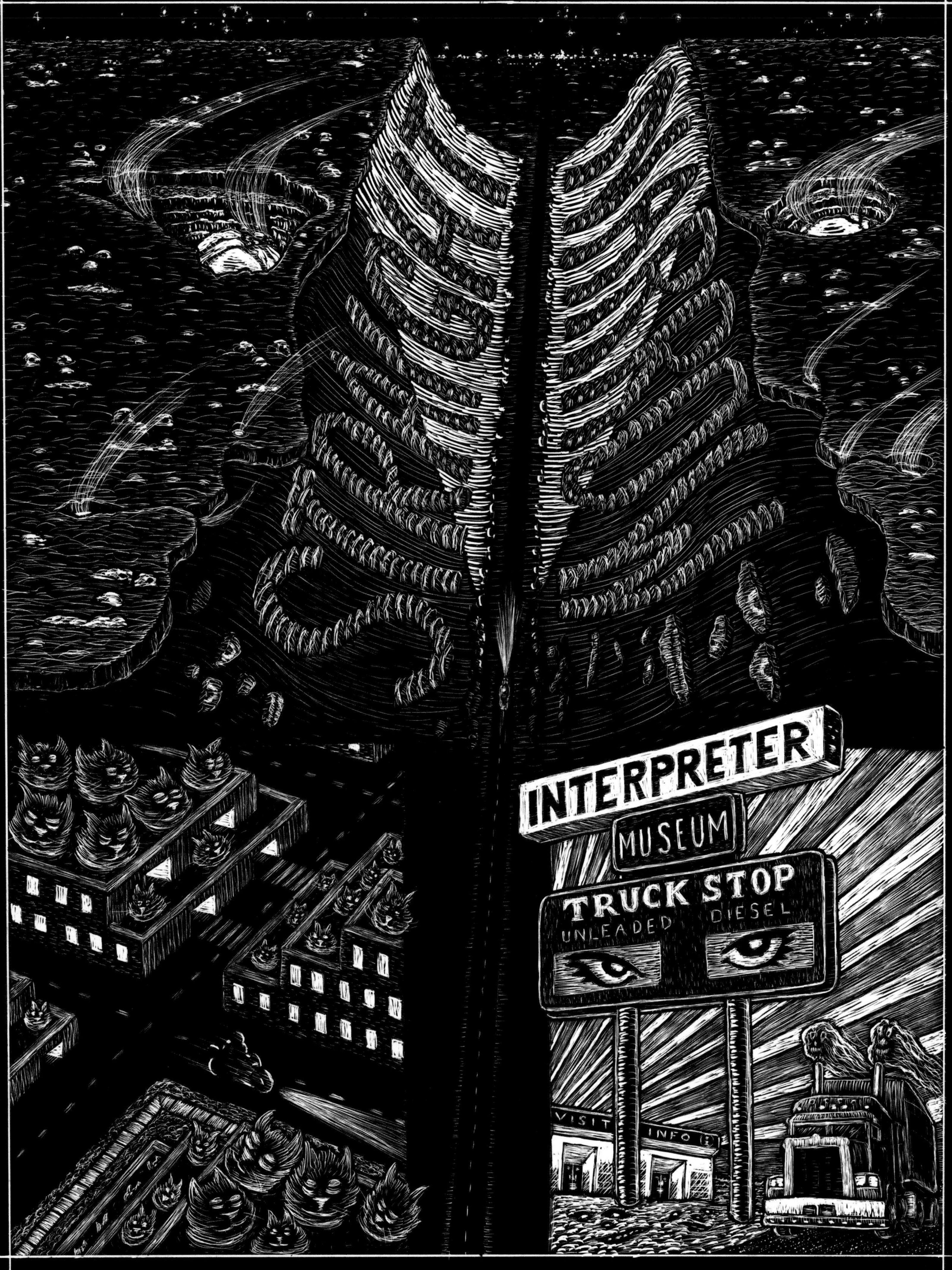
INTERPRETER
MUSEUM
TRUCK STOP
UNLEADED DIESEL
VISIT
INFO

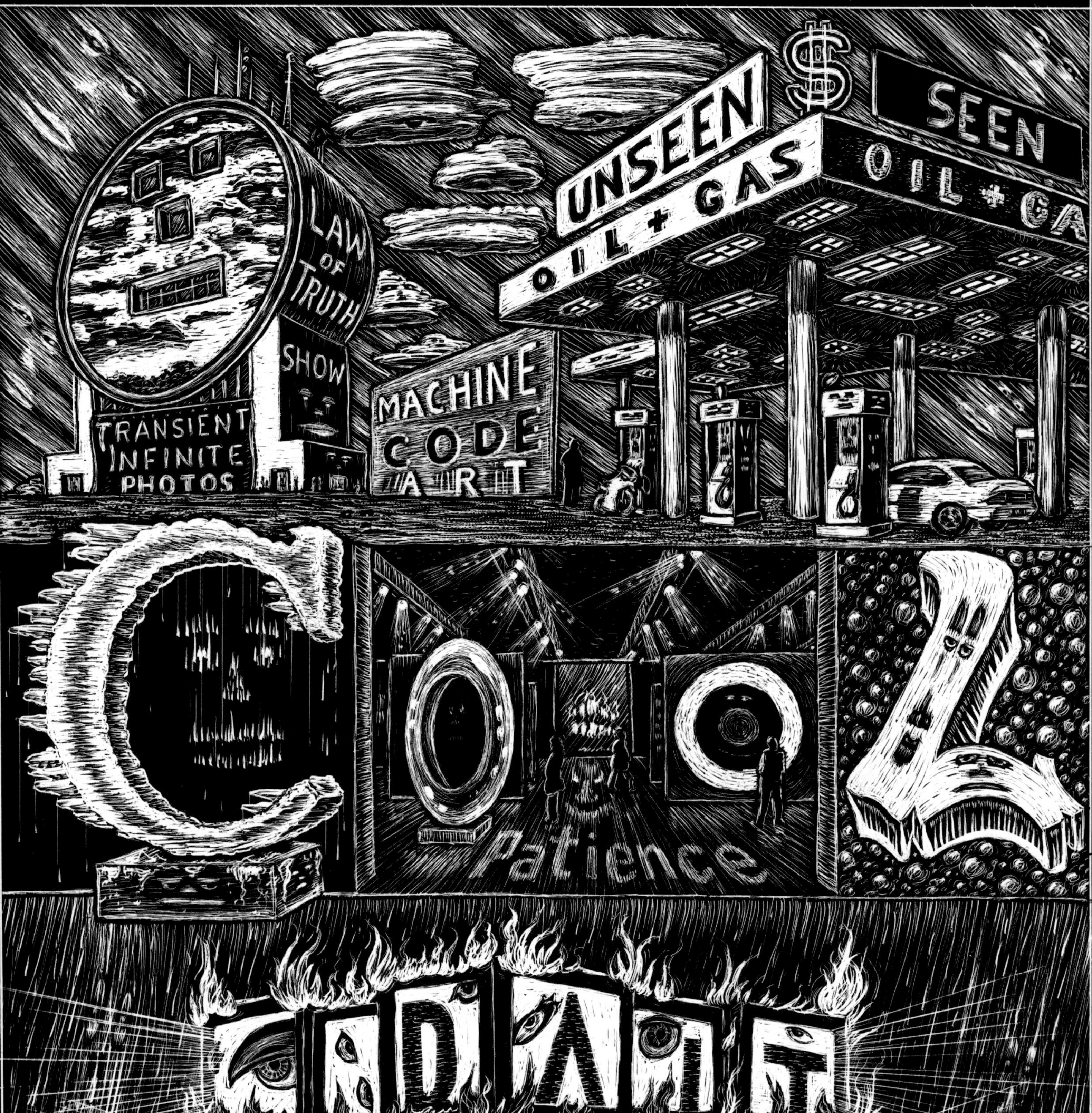
UNSEEN
OIL + GAS
SEEN
OIL + GA
LAW OF TRUTH
SHOW
TRANSIENT INFINITE PHOTOS
MACHINE CODE ART
Patience
CATCH THE

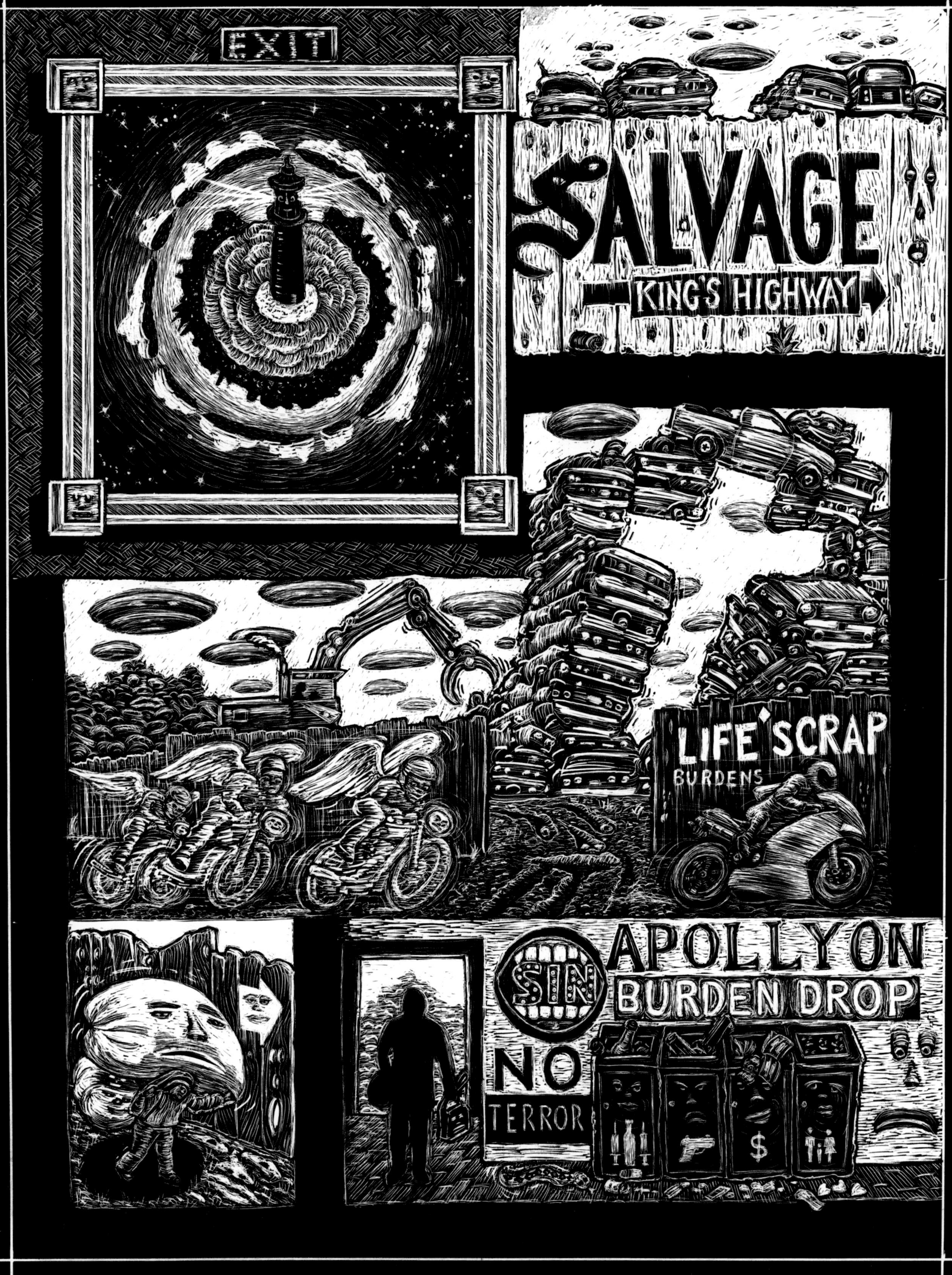
EXIT
SALVAGE
KING'S HIGHWAY
LIFE'SCRAP
BURDENS
SIN
APOLLYON
BURDEN DROP
NO
TERROR
$

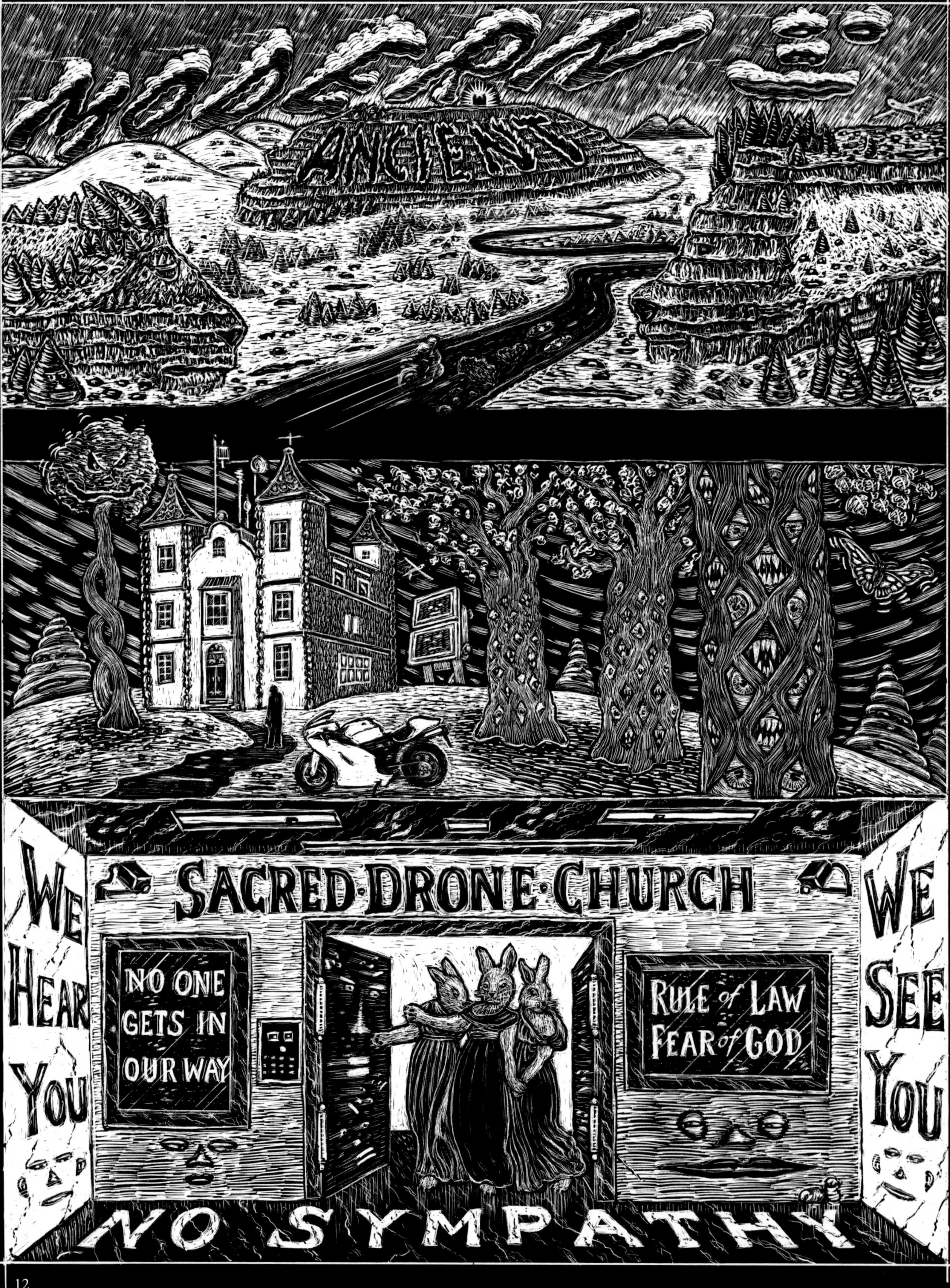

MODERN
ANCIENT
SACRED·DRONE·CHURCH
WE HEAR YOU
NO ONE GETS IN OUR WAY
RULE of LAW FEAR of GOD
WE SEE YOU
NO SYMPATHY

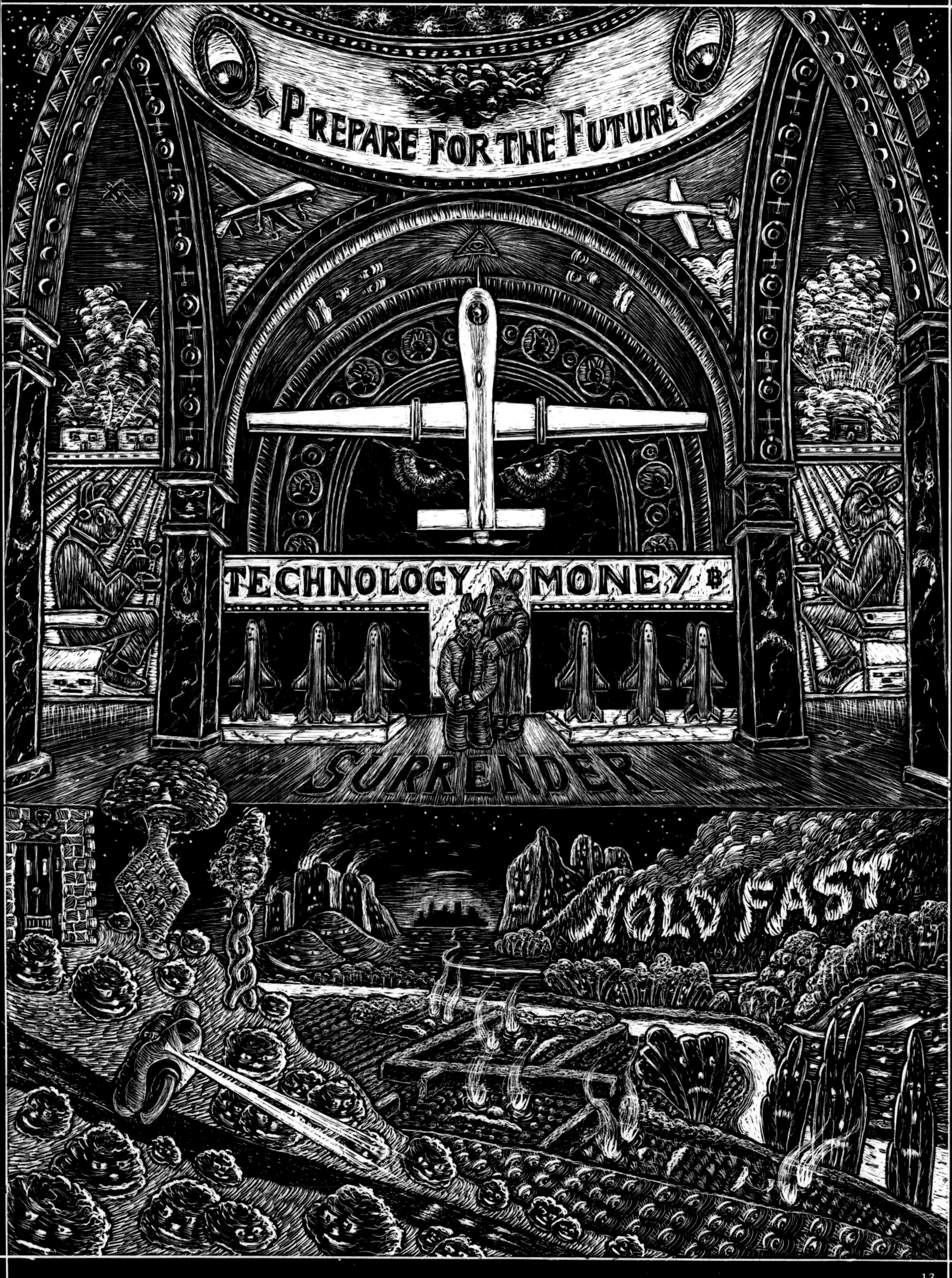

PREPARE FOR THE FUTURE
TECHNOLOGY
MONEY ฿
SURRENDER
HOLD FAST

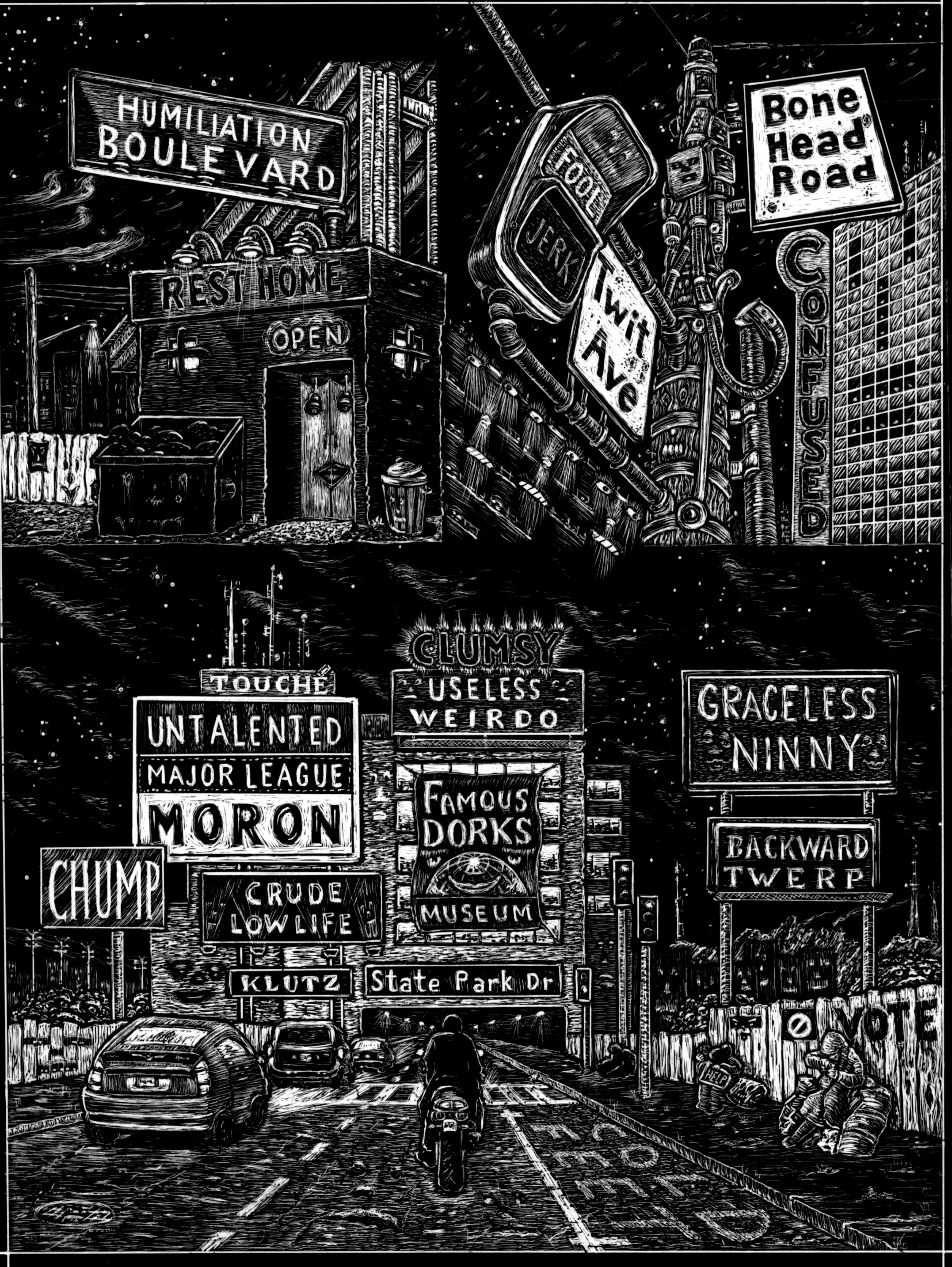
HUMILIATION BOULEVARD
REST HOME
OPEN
FOOL
JERK
Twit Ave
Bone Head Road
CONFUSED
CLUMSY
TOUCHÉ
UNTALENTED
MAJOR LEAGUE
MORON
USELESS WEIRDO
FAMOUS DORKS
MUSEUM
GRACELESS NINNY
BACKWARD TWERP
CHUMP
CRUDE LOWLIFE
KLUTZ
State Park Dr
VOTE
HELP

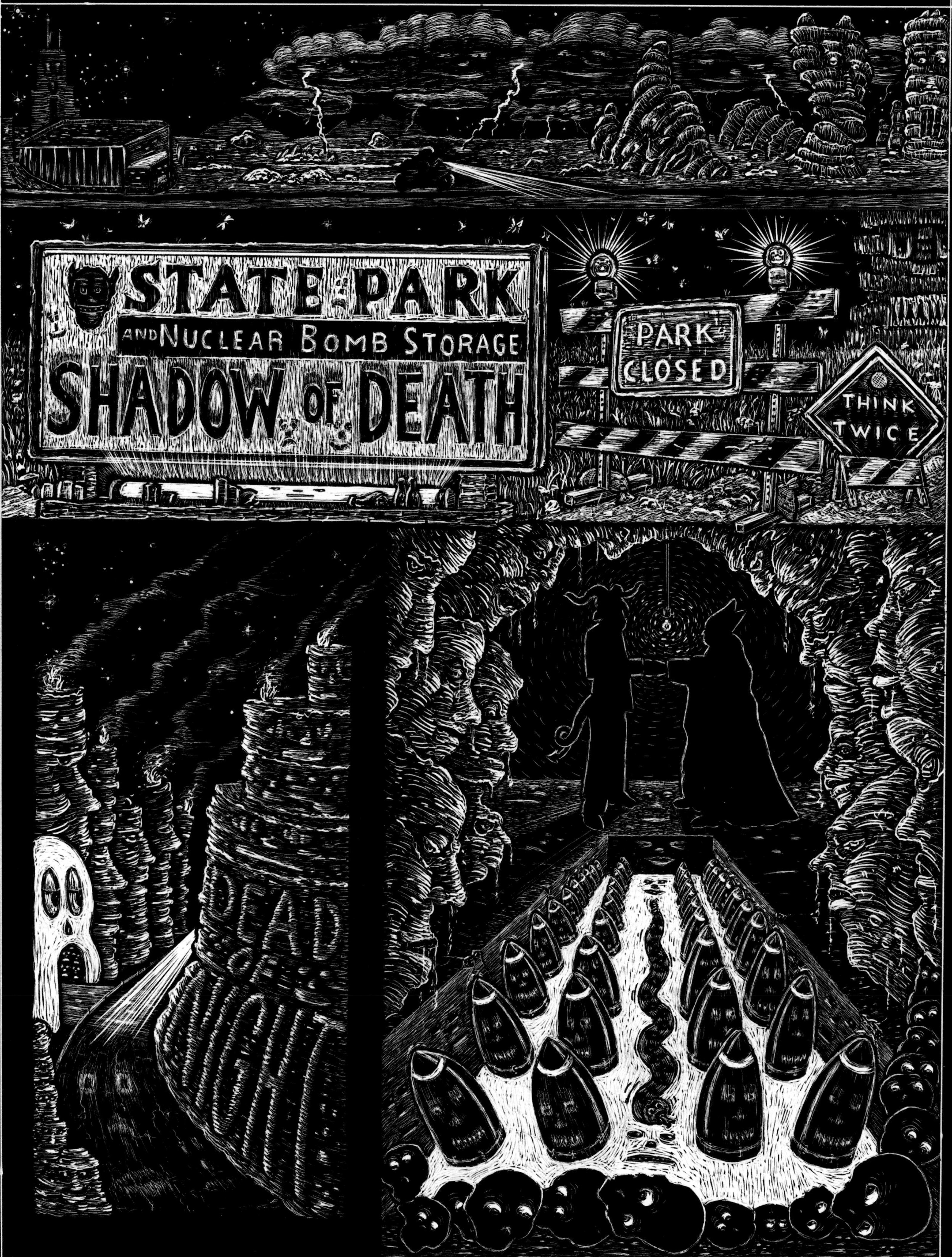
STATE PARK
AND NUCLEAR BOMB STORAGE
SHADOW OF DEATH
PARK CLOSED
THINK TWICE
DEAD OF NIGHT

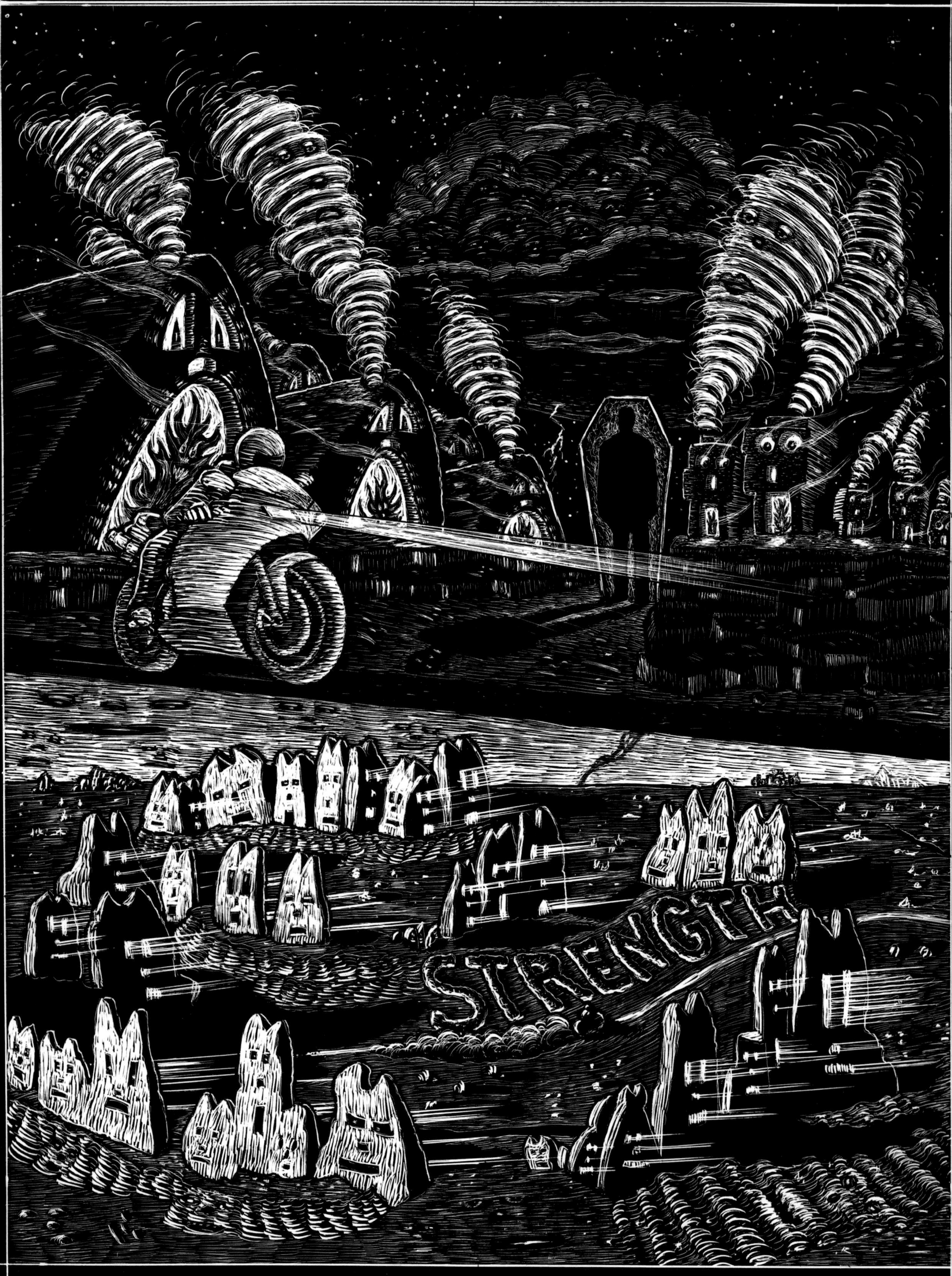
STRENGTH

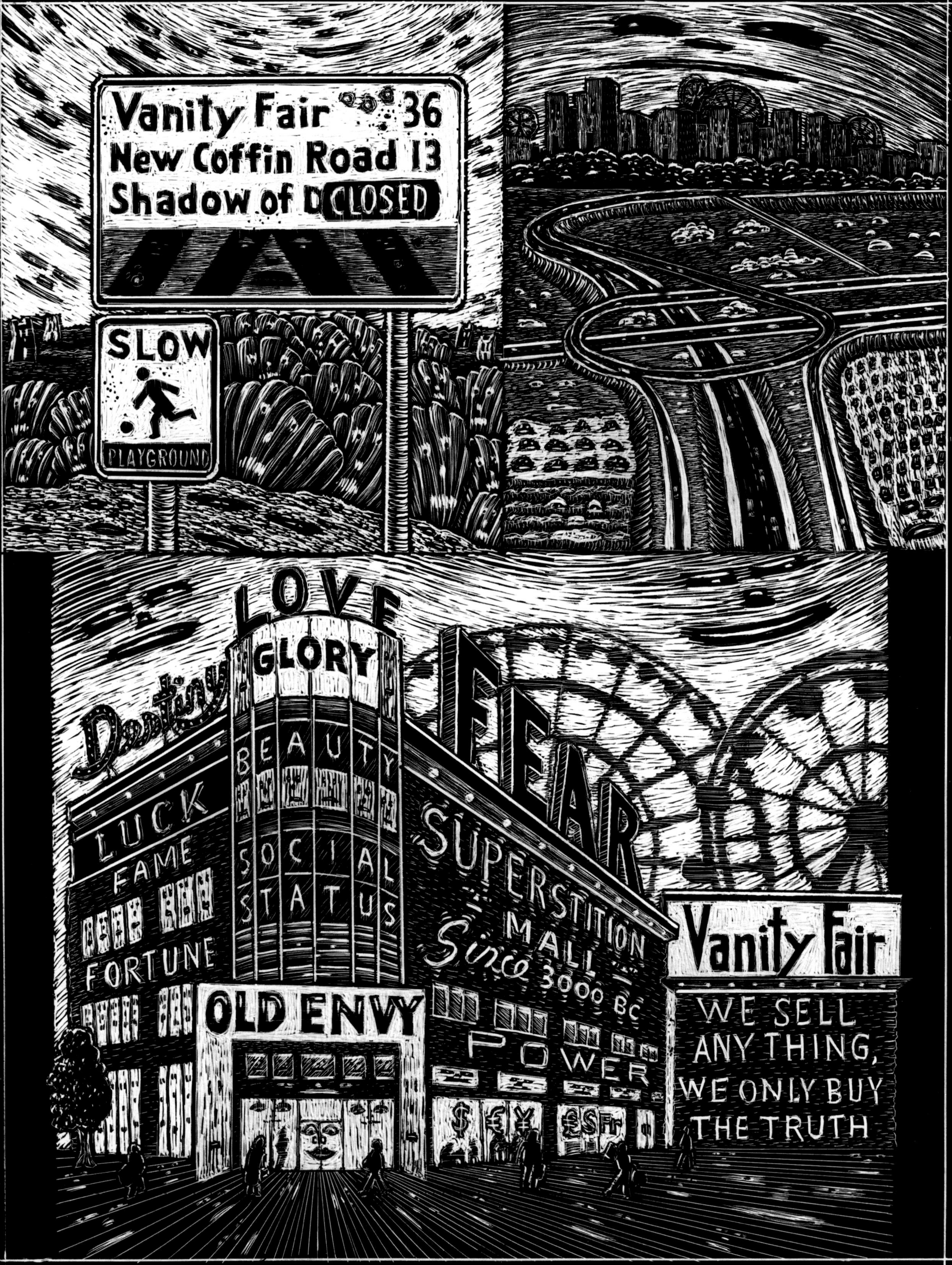
Vanity Fair 36
New Coffin Road 13
Shadow of D CLOSED
SLOW
PLAYGROUND
LOVE
GLORY
Destiny
BEAUTY
FEAR
LUCK
FAME
SOCIAL STATUS
SUPERSTITION
MALL
Since 3000 BC
FORTUNE
OLD ENVY
POWER
Vanity Fair
WE SELL ANY THING, WE ONLY BUY THE TRUTH

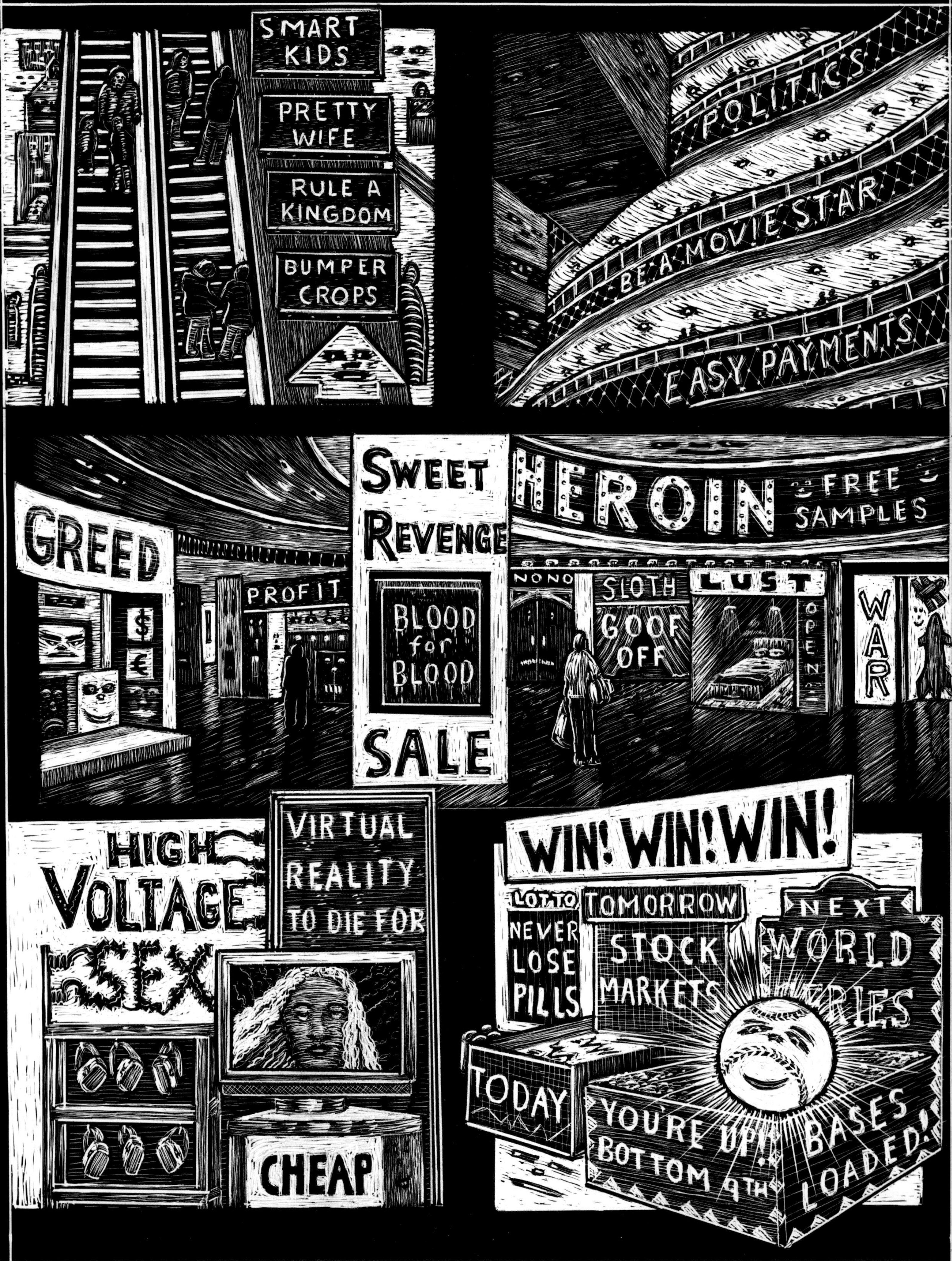
SMART KIDS
PRETTY WIFE
RULE A KINGDOM
BUMPER CROPS
POLITICS
BE A MOVIE STAR
EASY PAYMENTS
GREED
$
€
PROFIT
SWEET REVENGE
BLOOD for BLOOD
SALE
HEROIN
FREE SAMPLES
NONO
SLOTH
GOOF OFF
LUST
OPEN
WAR
HIGH VOLTAGE
SEX
VIRTUAL REALITY TO DIE FOR
CHEAP
WIN! WIN! WIN!
LOTTO
NEVER LOSE PILLS
TOMORROW
STOCK MARKETS
NEXT WORLD SERIES
TODAY
YOU'RE UP! BOTTOM 9TH
BASES LOADED!

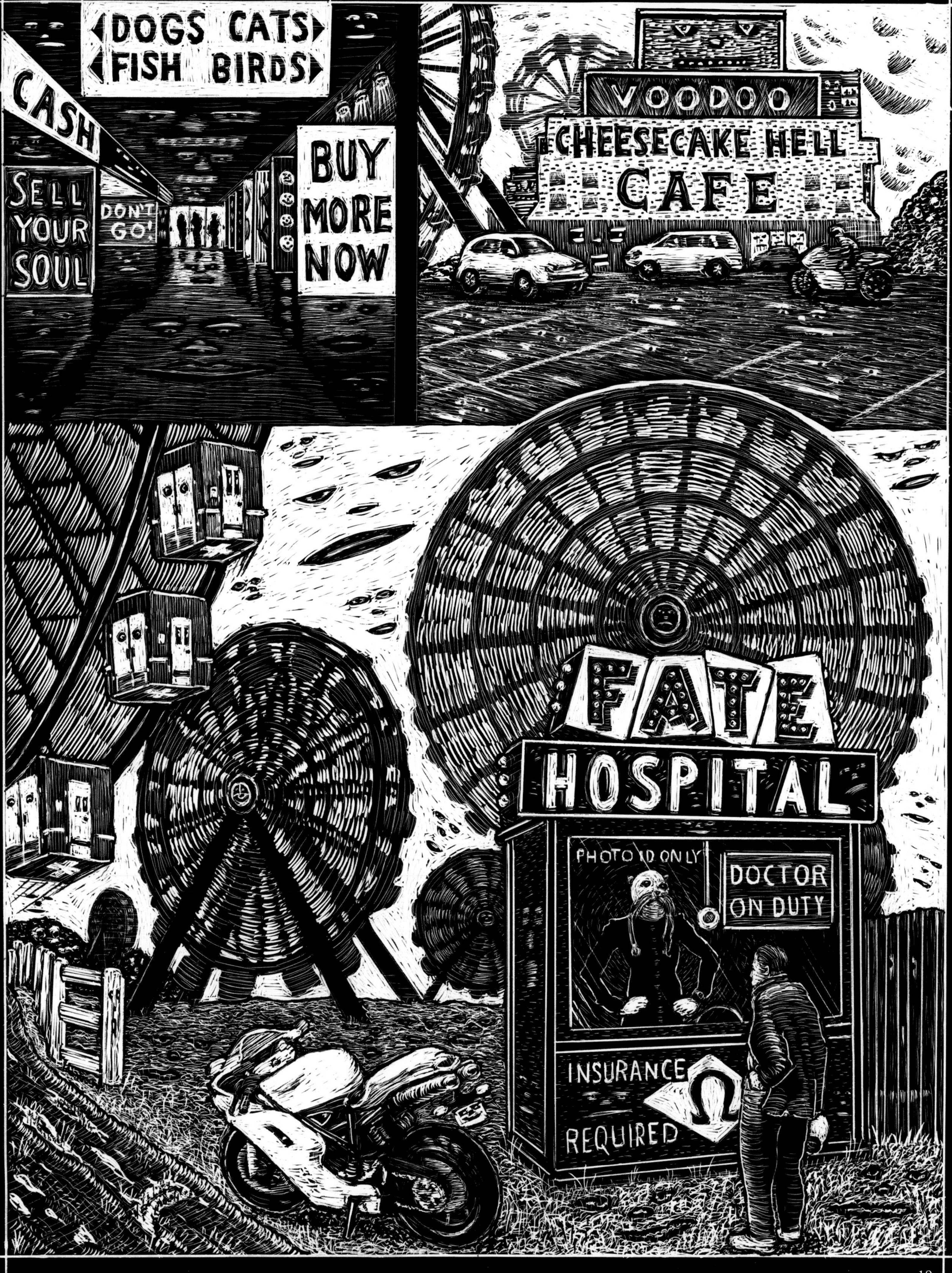

DOGS CATS
FISH BIRDS
CASH
SELL YOUR SOUL
DON'T GO!
BUY MORE NOW
VOODOO
CHEESECAKE HELL
CAFE
FATE
HOSPITAL
PHOTO ID ONLY
DOCTOR ON DUTY
INSURANCE
REQUIRED

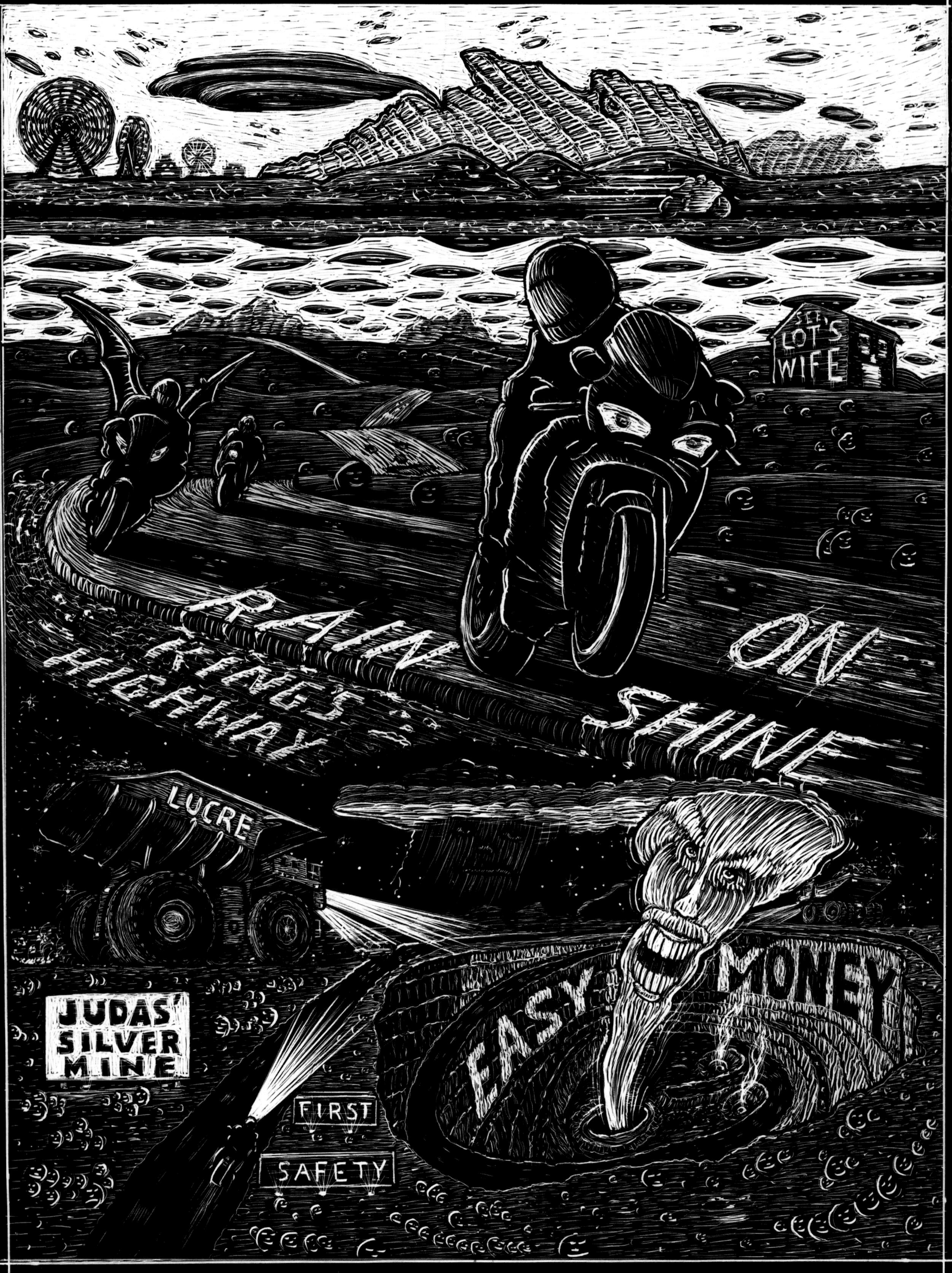
SEE
LOT'S
WIFE
RAIN ON
KING'S HIGHWAY
SHINE
LUCRE
EASY MONEY
JUDAS' SILVER MINE
FIRST
SAFETY

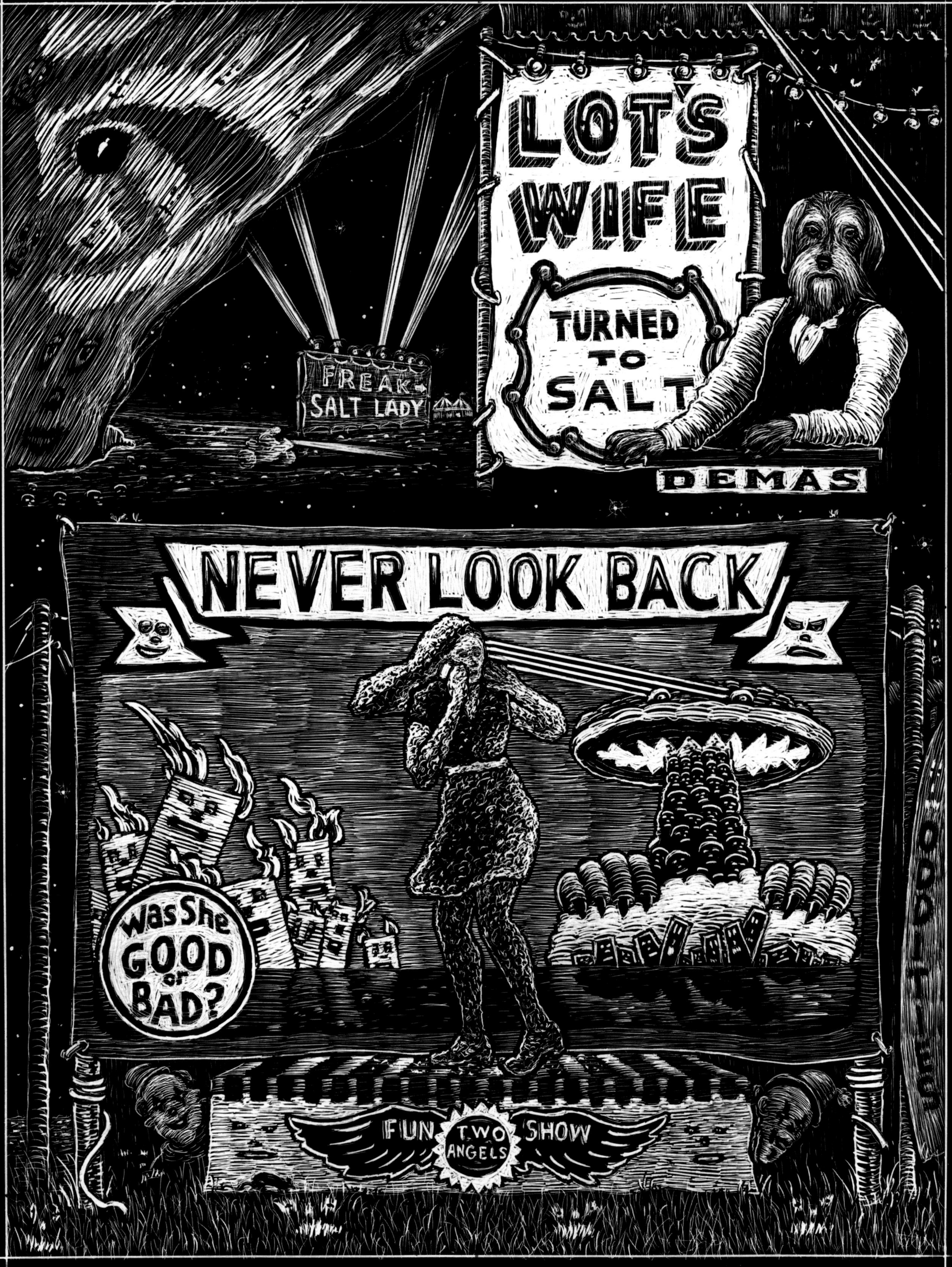
LOT'S WIFE
TURNED TO SALT
FREAK
SALT LADY
DEMAS
NEVER LOOK BACK
Was She GOOD or BAD?
FUN TWO ANGELS SHOW

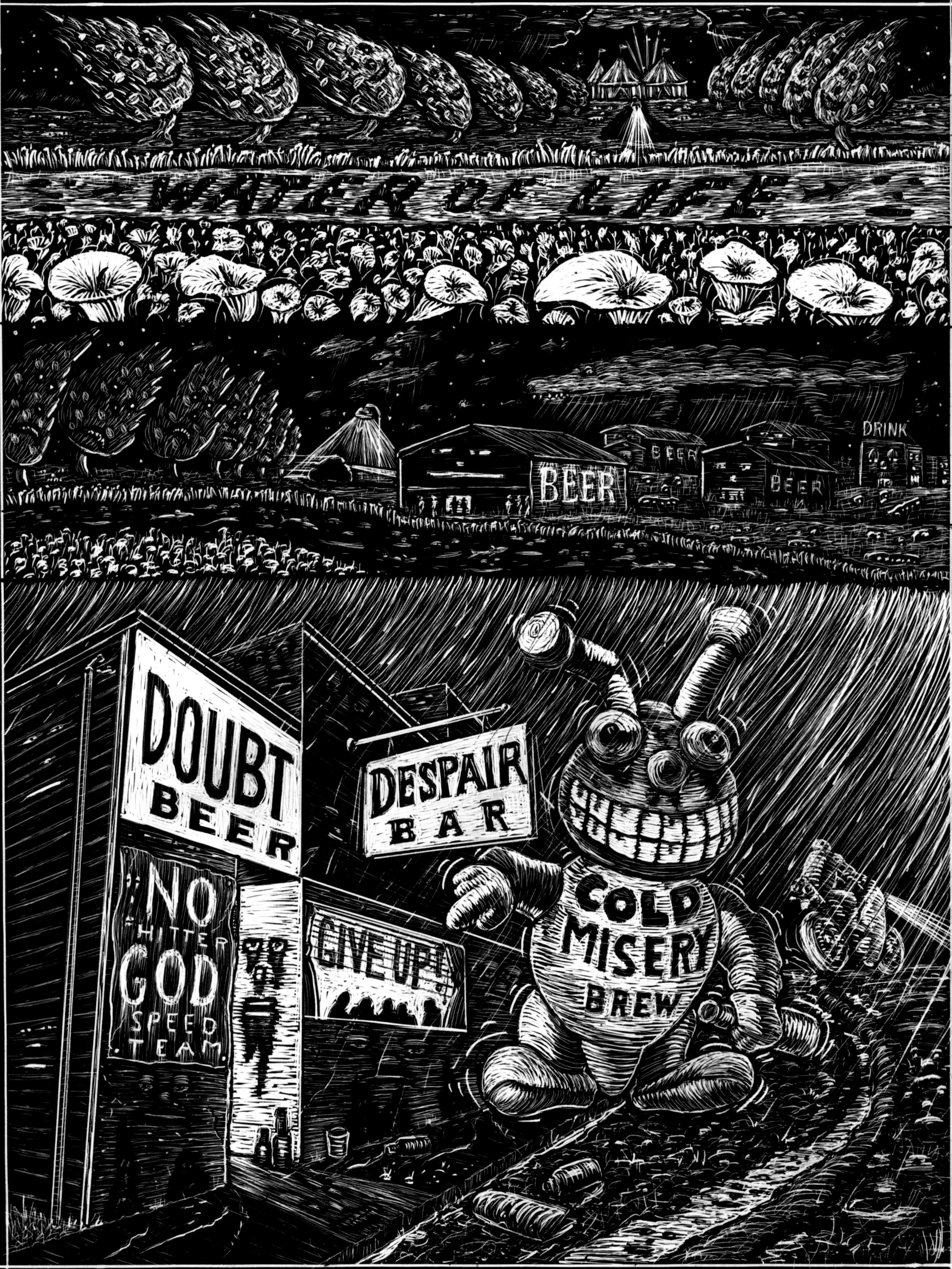
WATER OF LIFE
DRINK
BEER
BEER
BEER
DOUBT
BEER
DESPAIR
BAR
NO
HITTER
GOD
SPEED
TEAM
GIVE UP!
COLD
MISERY
BREW

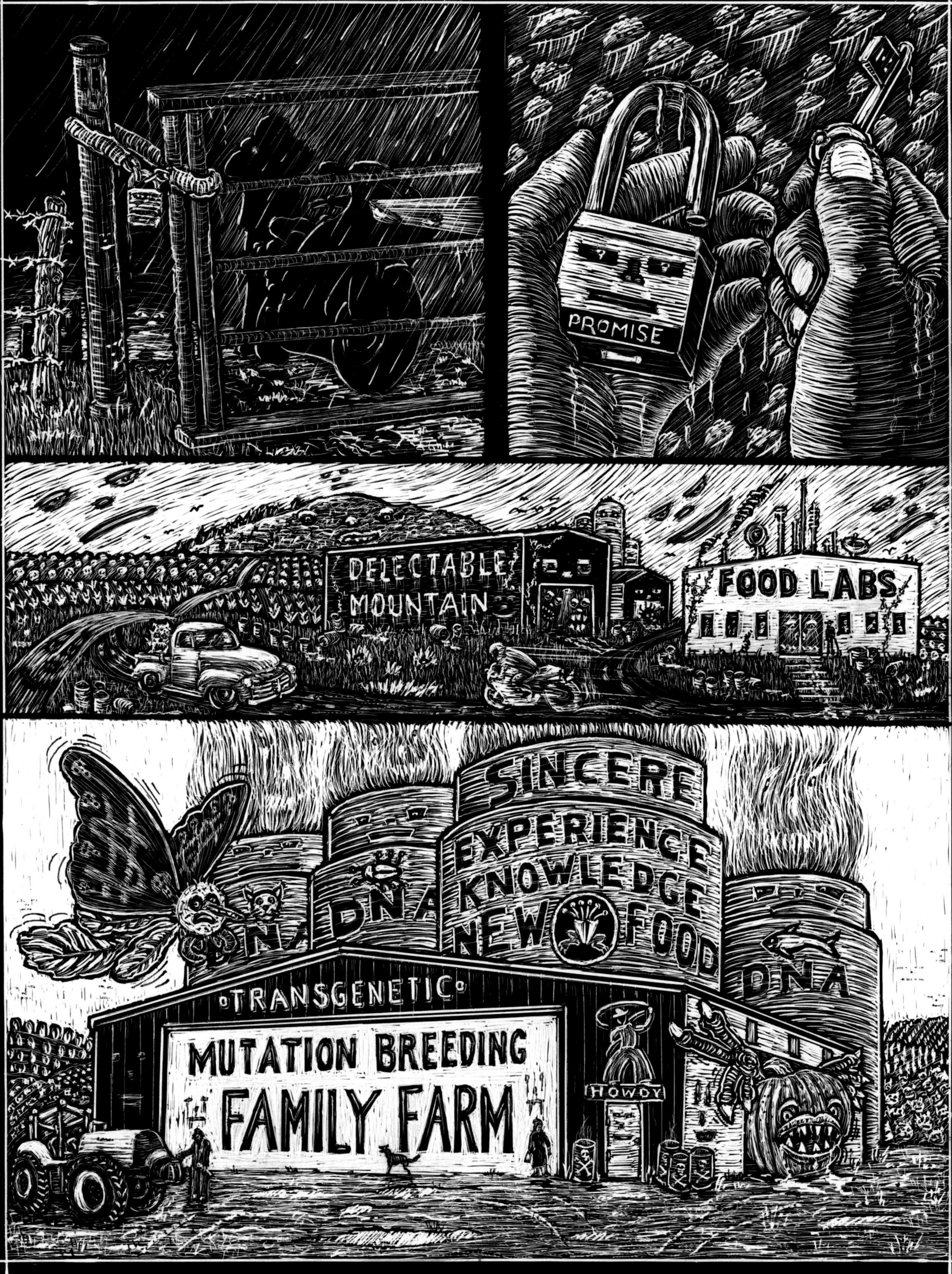
PROMISE
DELECTABLE MOUNTAIN
FOOD LABS
SINCERE
EXPERIENCE
KNOWLEDGE
NEW FOOD
DNA
DNA
DNA
TRANSGENETIC
MUTATION BREEDING
FAMILY FARM
HOWDY

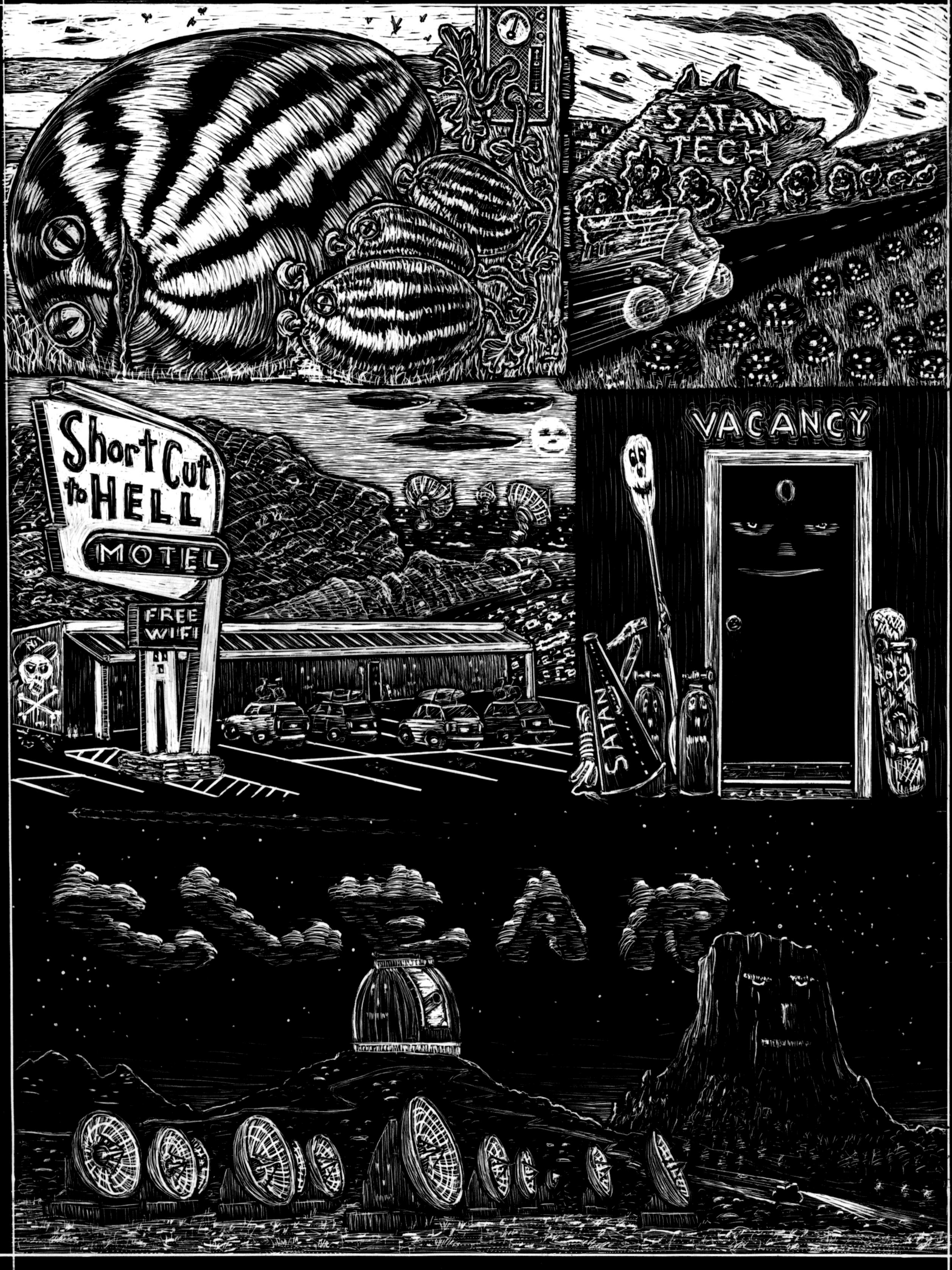
SATAN TECH
Short Cut to HELL
MOTEL
FREE WIFI
VACANCY
SATAN

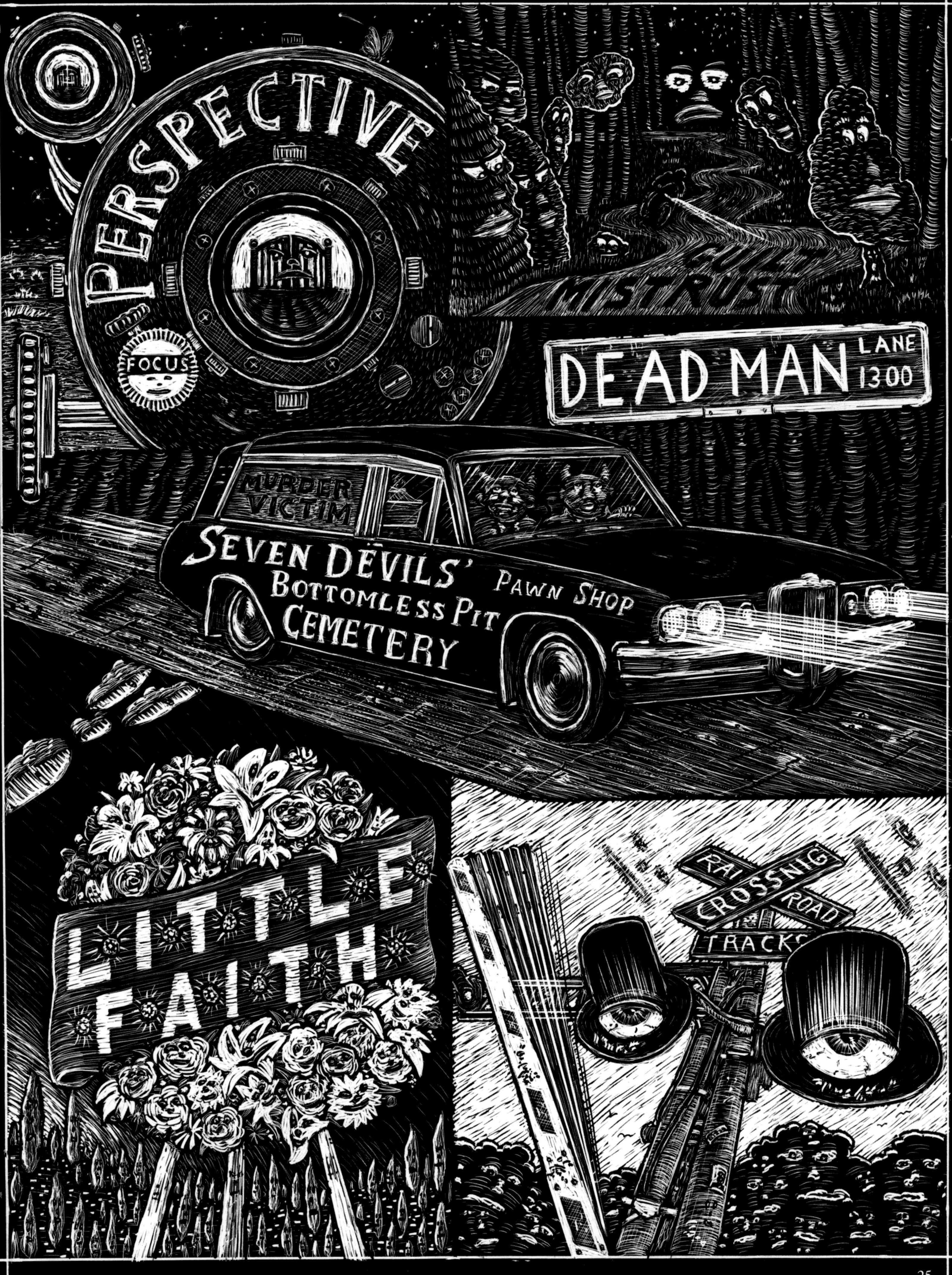
PERSPECTIVE
FOCUS
GUILT
MISTRUST
DEAD MAN LANE 1300
MURDER VICTIM
SEVEN DEVILS' PAWN SHOP
BOTTOMLESS PIT
CEMETERY
LITTLE FAITH
RAIL ROAD
CROSSNIG
TRACKS

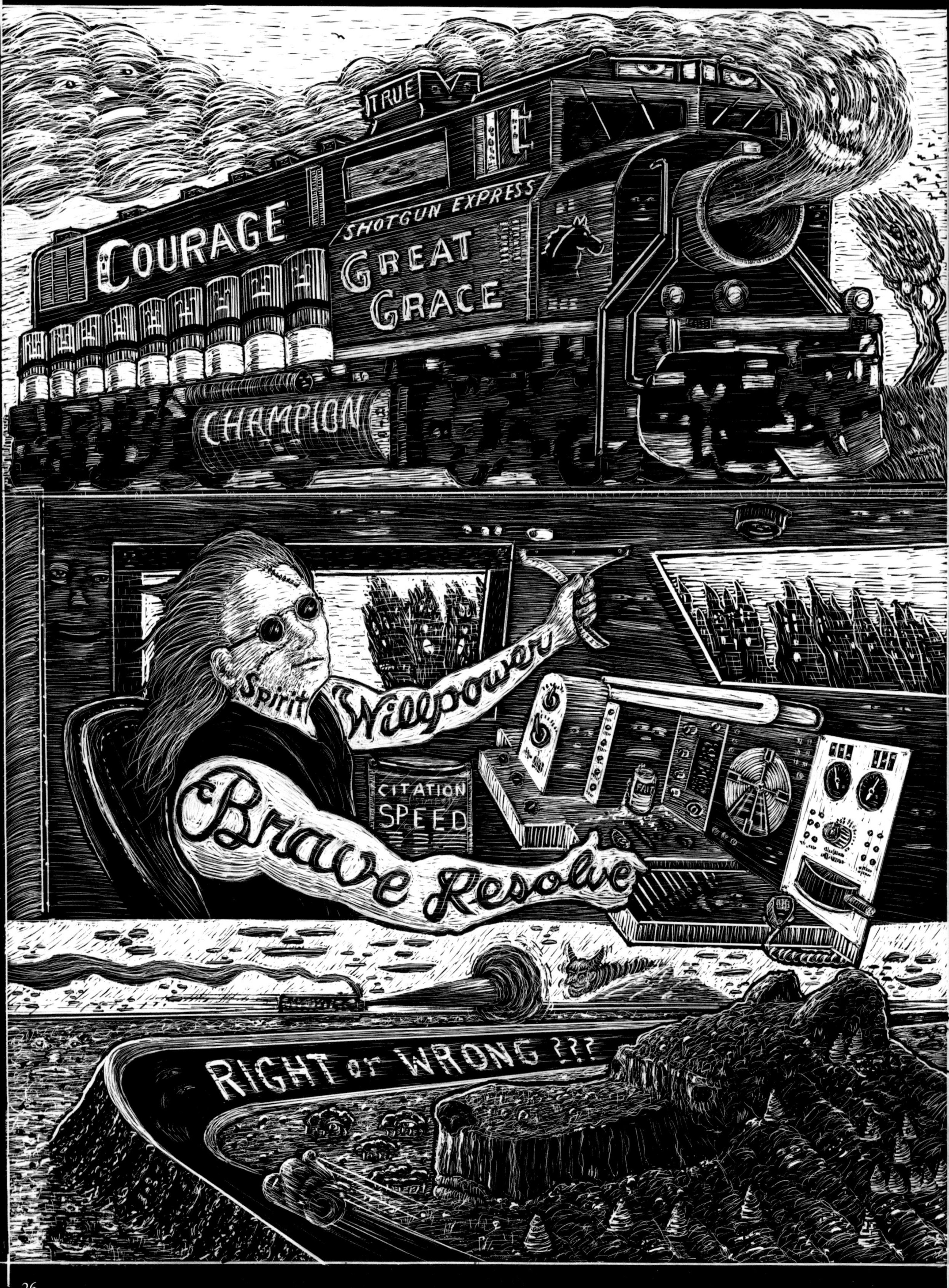
TRUE
COURAGE
SHOTGUN EXPRESS
GREAT
GRACE
CHAMPION
Spirit
Willpower
CITATION
SPEED
Brave Resolve
RIGHT or WRONG ???

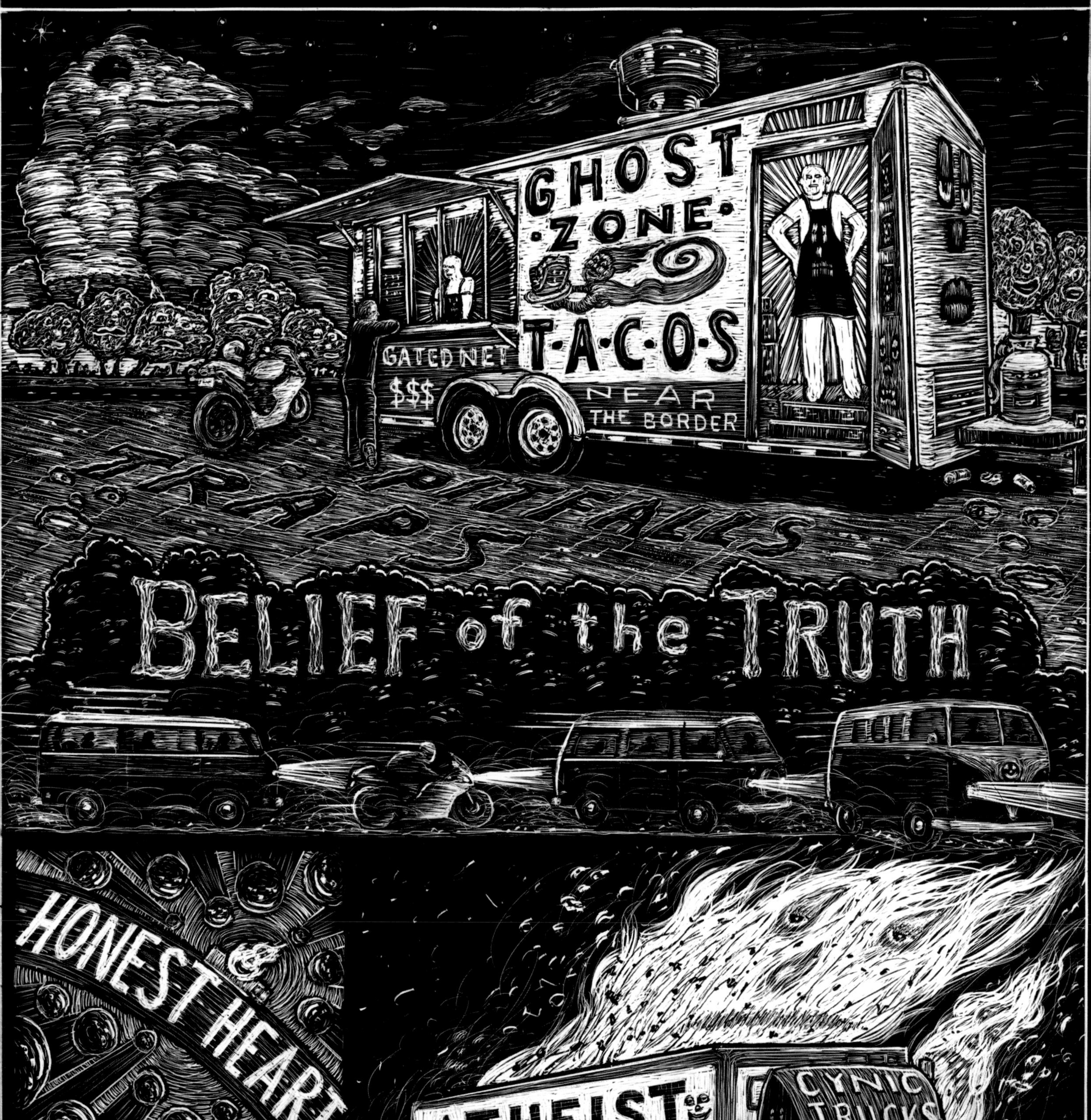
GHOST
·ZONE·
T·A·C·O·S
GATEDNET
$$$
NEAR
THE BORDER
BELIEF of the TRUTH
HONEST HEART
ATHEIST
VAN LINES
UNBELIEVABLE!
CYNIC
TRUCKS
SKEPTICS
TRANSPORT
World to Come
RUN

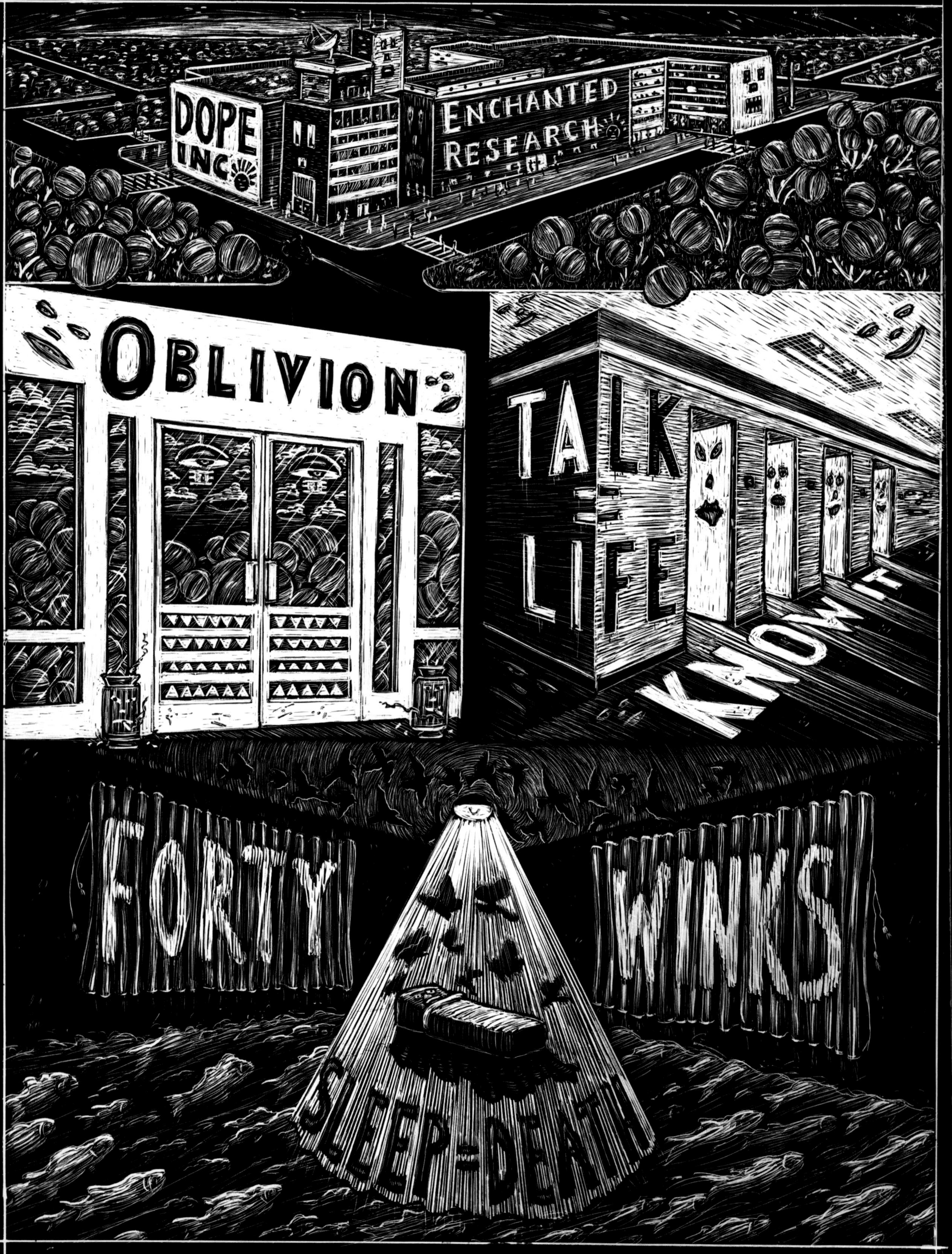
DOPE INC
ENCHANTED RESEARCH
OBLIVION
TALK
LIFE
KNOW IT
FORTY
WINKS
SLEEP=DEATH

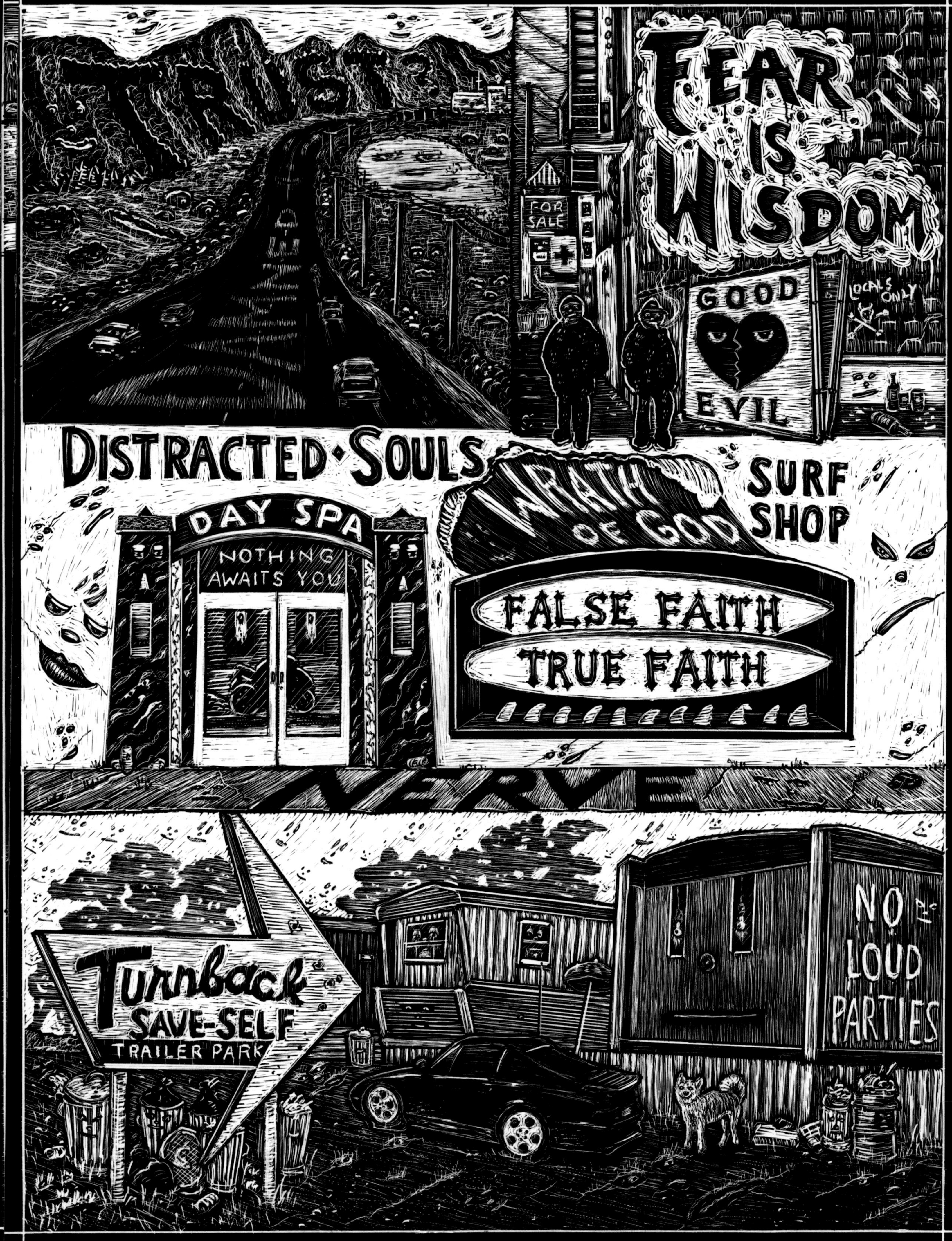

TRUST
FEAR IS WISDOM
FOR SALE
GOOD EVIL
LOCALS ONLY
DISTRACTED SOULS
DAY SPA
NOTHING AWAITS YOU
WRATH OF GOD
SURF SHOP
FALSE FAITH
TRUE FAITH
NERVE
Turnback SAVE-SELF
TRAILER PARK
NO LOUD PARTIES

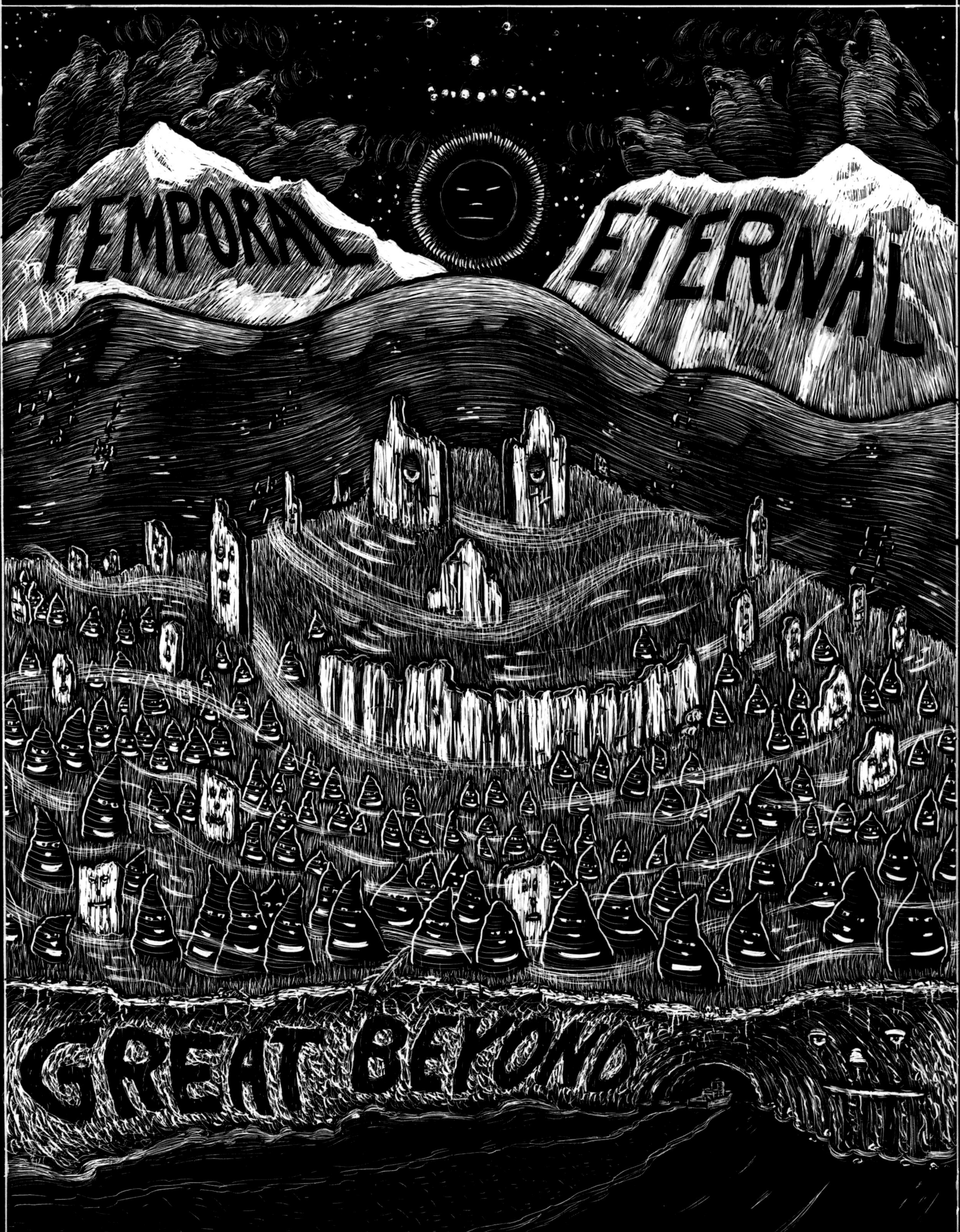
TEMPORAL
ETERNAL
GREAT BEYOND

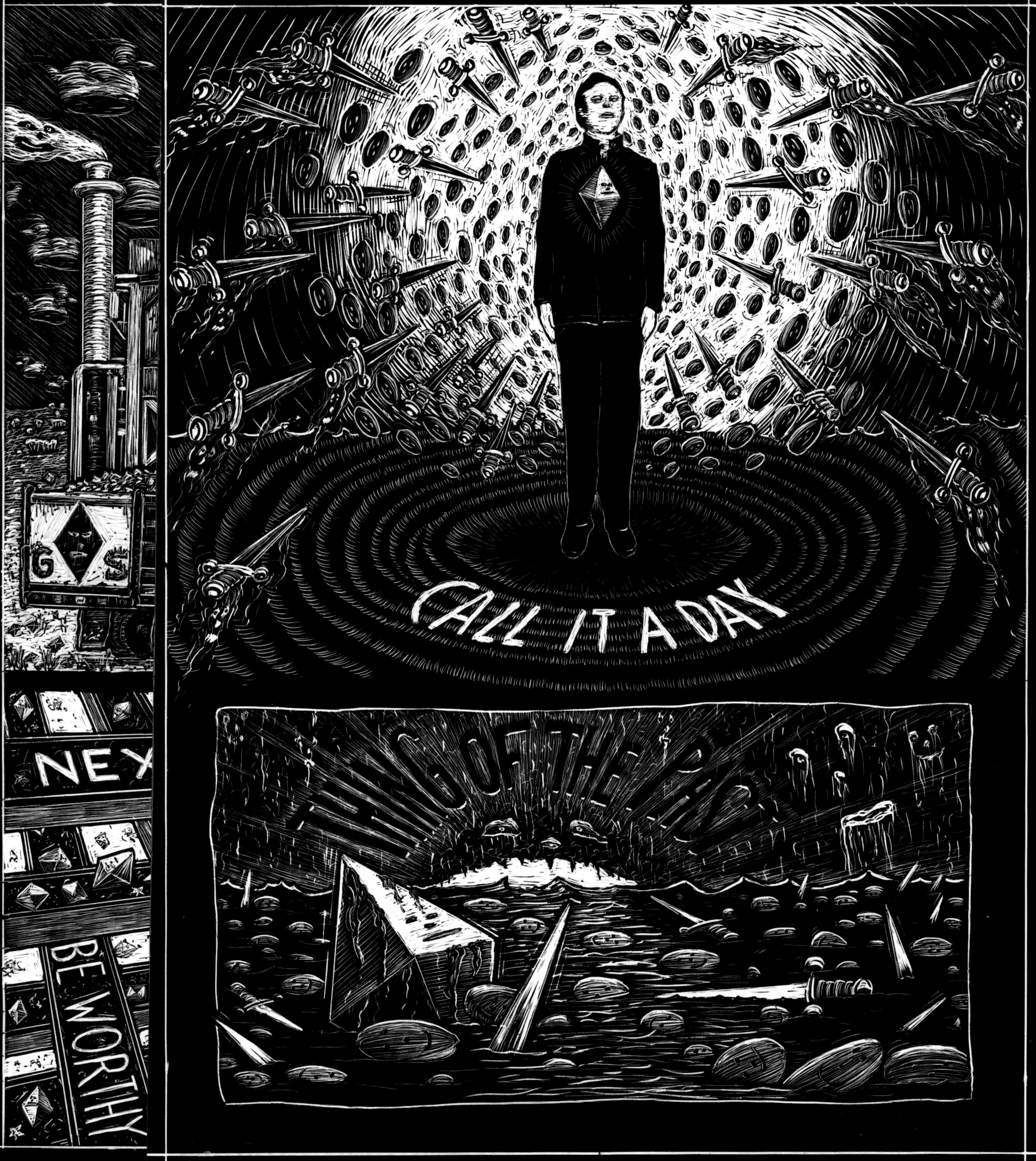

G S
NEX
BE WORTHY
CALL IT A DAY
OF THE

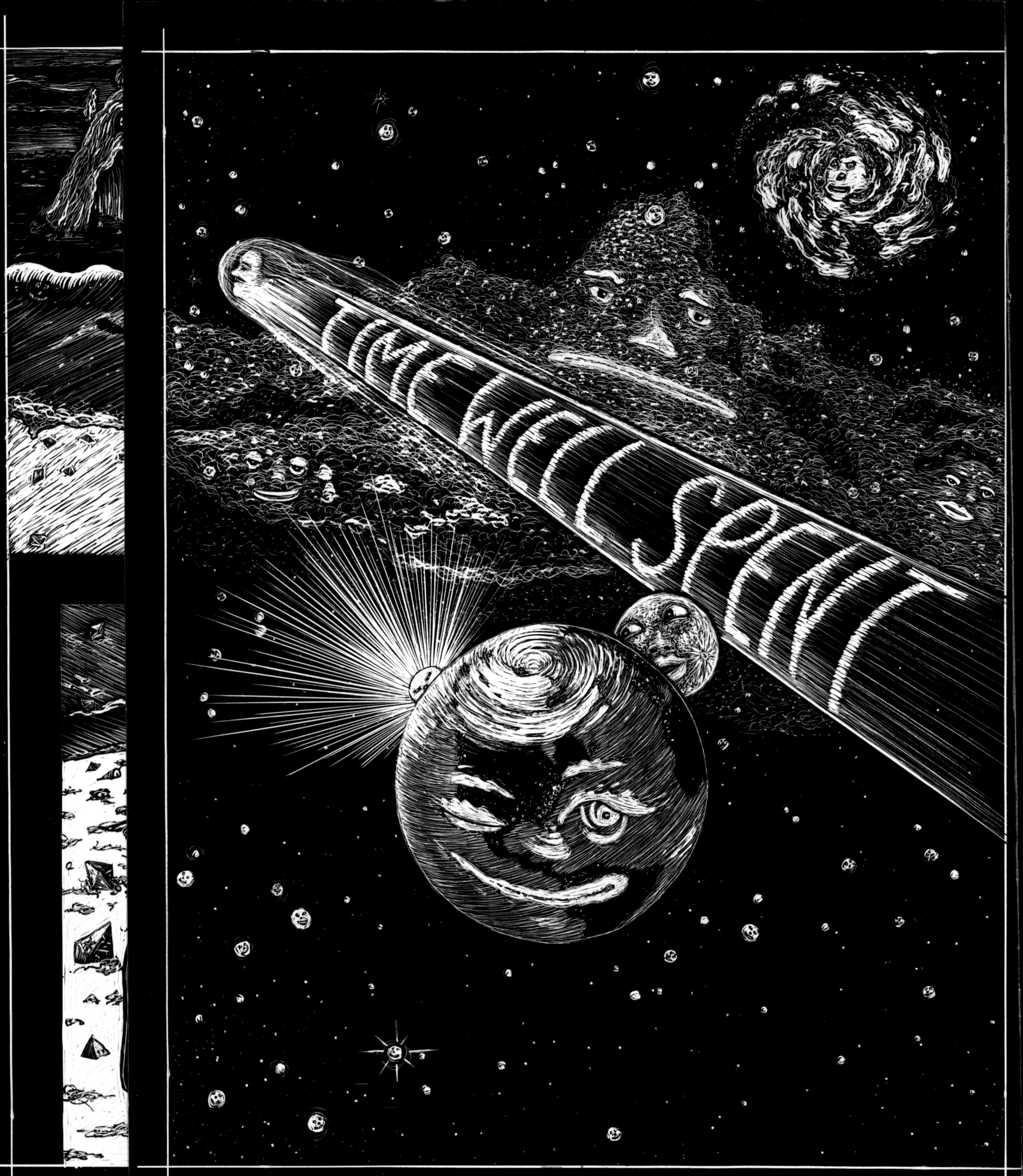
TIME WELL SPENT